SPECTRUM®

Science

Grade 7

Spectrum®

An imprint of Carson-Dellosa Publishing LLC
Greensboro, North Carolina

Spectrum
An imprint of Carson-Dellosa Publishing LLC
P.O. Box 35665
Greensboro, NC 27425 USA

ISBN 978-1-4838-1171-0

01-227147811

Table of Contents

Chapter 4 Earth and Space Science

Chapter 5 Science and Technology

Lesson 1.1   Keys to Unlocking the World

discipline: an area of knowledge or study

unreliable: can't be trusted or depended on

formulas: mathematical equations expressed in symbols

velocity: speed, or the distance traveled in a set amount of time

statistics: math that deals with the collection, organization, and analysis of numerical facts

Like other areas of modern life, computers have become one of the most widely used tools in every scientific discipline. A good scientist must know how to use a word processing program, the Internet, and any software that helps his or her research.

The scientific method:
1. Ask a question.
2. Form a hypothesis.
3. Design and conduct an experiment.
4. Draw conclusions based on the results.
5. Share the details and results of the experiment with other scientists.

What skills do you need to be a good scientist?

Science begins with curiosity. Taking an interest in the world around you and asking questions about how and why things happen is just the first step, though. Scientists depend on a wide range of skills and tools to help them investigate and discover the answers.

As a scientist, you'll need to know how to use certain tools. Whether it's a scale, a microscope, a laser, or a Bunsen burner, you need to be familiar with each tool's function and how it's used safely. Laboratories can be places for discovery, but they can also be places of danger. Being careful, precise, and safe are a scientist's top priorities in the lab.

The specific tools scientists use each day depend on which scientific **discipline** they're involved in and the kind of research they're doing. However, certain skills are used nearly every day in every kind of science.

One of the most basic skills is careful observation. Observation is the key to all good scientific research. Whether you're conducting experiments, studying animals in the wild, or digging through the ground in search of ancient bones, you need to observe everything closely and take detailed notes. An event that seems minor or unimportant when it happens may turn out to be the reason an experiment fails or succeeds. If you don't bother to record the event—or even notice it—then your research will be incomplete and your results will be **unreliable**.

Another important skill used by all scientists is math. Physicists and chemists, for example, need to be familiar with a wide variety of mathematical **formulas**. Sometimes, they're easy—**velocity** is distance divided by time, or $v = d/t$. Sometimes, they're more complex—the surface area of a sphere is four times pi times the radius squared, or $s = 4\pi r^2$.

Other scientists, like biologists and ecologists, commonly use **statistics** to study and compare the data they recorded while making observations.

A scientist must be skilled in language and communication, as well. Remember, science is an ongoing process that depends on sharing research and results. Each new discovery builds on the discoveries made by scientists in the past and adds to the collective body of scientific knowledge. If you can't communicate well, how will you be able to explain to other scientists the amazing discoveries you've made?

Circle the letter of the best answer to the question below.

1. Certain skills are important to every scientist. Which of the following is not one of them?

    a. typing on a keyboard

    b. performing mathematical calculations

    c. using a microscope

    d. communicating

Write your answers on the lines below.

2. Why is careful observation such an important part of being a scientist?

    _____

3. Imagine that you develop a hypothesis and design an experiment, but your experiment shows that your hypothesis is incorrect. Should you still publish the results of your experiment? Why or why not?

    _____

    _____

    _____

4. The word *interdisciplinary* means "involving more than one field of knowledge or study." Explain why a good scientist needs to have interdisciplinary skills.

    _____

    _____

    _____

What's Next?

The latest and most up-to-date scientific research isn't usually found in books. Scientific magazines, called *journals*, are often the first place scientists publish their research and results. This way, other scientists around the world can review the methods that were used and draw conclusions about how reliable the results are. Though you probably will not find scientific journals at your local bookstore, you will find magazines that describe some of the latest scientific discoveries and news.

The Human Hobbits

Homo sapiens: the species to which modern human beings belong; characterized by a large brain, language, reasoning, and the ability to walk on two legs

microcephaly: abnormally small head and brain

There were other interesting findings in the cave where the skull was discovered. Scientists found evidence of fire, as well as tools that would have been used by someone the size of the hobbit. The dates of these artifacts matched the dates that hobbits would have lived. The use of tools and fire indicated that *Homo floresiensis* was capable of problem solving—skills that would have seemed too advanced for the size of its brain.

How small were the early ancestors of human beings?

If you've ever read any books by J. R. R. Tolkien or seen the movies based on his books, then you've probably heard of hobbits—small, round, human-like creatures with pointy ears. The hobbit was born in Tolkien's imagination and has no resemblance to any actual living being, past or present. That is, at least, until a few years ago.

In 2004, researchers found the remains of a small relative of human beings in a cave on the Indonesian island of Flores. At first, they believed it belonged to a child. When they examined it further, though, they saw that there was too much wear on the teeth for it to have been a child. Other features of the skull made the scientists think that it was several million years old. It had a sloping forehead, unlike modern human beings, as well as thick eyebrow ridges and a small chin. They believed the skull belonged to a 30-year-old female who was about 3 feet 4 inches tall and weighed 55 pounds—about the size of a modern four year old. Her brain would have been about one-quarter the size of a modern adult brain.

The biggest surprise came when the scientists dated the remains to only about 18,000 years old. This small species of human existed at the same time as ***Homo sapiens***, the species that modern human beings belong to. Until the discovery of *Homo floresiensis*—or "the hobbit," as it was nicknamed—it was believed that all other species of early human beings were extinct by the time *Homo sapiens* walked the planet.

There has been much controversy since the discovery. Some scientists believe that the hobbit isn't a separate species of human being. Instead, they think that the specimen that was discovered had **microcephaly**. The remains of seven more individuals have been found on Flores, though, and they are all the same size. It would be odd for so many people in a small area to have had the same condition. This supports the idea that the hobbits are actually a separate species.

Early in 2007, skull casts were done of modern human beings with microcephaly. These casts were compared with the ancient remains. The researchers who conducted the study felt sure that the hobbits did not have this condition. As research in Flores continues, scientists on both sides of the debate hope to find evidence that supports their theories.

Write your answers on the lines below.

1. How was *Homo floresiensis* different in appearance from *Homo sapiens*?

    _____

    _____

2. Why were researchers surprised to find out how old the remains of the hobbit were?

    _____

    _____

3. Why did scientists first believe that the skull they found belonged to a child? Why did they change their opinions?

    _____

    _____

4. Why was the scientists' discovery of tools and fire in the cave where the hobbit was found significant?

    _____

    _____

5. Using the selection to illustrate your point, explain why it is necessary for scientists to be open minded and to be willing to adjust their beliefs as new information becomes available.

    _____

    _____

    _____

6. Why did scientists make skull casts of modern individuals with microcephaly?

    _____

7. In your opinion, is *Homo floresiensis* a separate human species? Why or why not?

    _____

    _____

anthropology: the study of human life and culture

archaeology: the study of human life and cultures of the past, using fossils and artifacts

hominid: the biological family that includes human beings and primates, in both present and extinct forms

Mary Leakey was a shy but careful scientist. Louis Leakey's outgoing personality, however, helped interest others in their work and to raise funds that allowed them to continue their research.

Richard Leakey (Louis and Mary's son), his wife Meave, and daughter Louise have all carried on the family tradition and are respected paleontologists.

Louis Leakey was fascinated by the study of primates. He helped primatologist Jane Goodall get her start and begin her long-term observation of wild chimpanzees. He also assisted other scientists, such as Dian Fossey, establish studies of primates.

Why were the contributions of the Leakeys so important to the study of early humanity?

Louis Leakey grew up in British East Africa in the early 1900s. He discovered his first fossils as an adolescent, which led to his lifelong passion for **anthropology** and **archaeology**.

Before Louis began his career, it was widely believed that the earliest human beings had lived in Asia. Louis was able to convince the scientific community that the first human beings evolved in Africa instead. As a result, other scientists refocused their attentions on Africa.

In the 1920s, Louis began leading expeditions to Olduvai River Gorge in modern-day Tanzania. There, he found animal fossils, as well as Stone Age tools. In 1948, he and his wife, Mary, made one of their most important finds—a skull they dated at 20 million years old. The Leakeys believed the skull to belong to an early human ancestor. The skull is not considered by modern experts to be a direct human ancestor, but it is still an important piece of the puzzle of human origins.

Many of the Leakeys' significant finds are attributed to Mary Leakey. Mary was a talented archaeologist at a time when few women had careers in science. In 1959, she found a **hominid** skull that she and Louis dated at 1.75 million years old. The oldest human remains found in Asia were only several thousand years old, so this supported the theory of Africa as the "cradle of humanity." A couple of years later, Mary found another skull of an ancient human ancestor. It was unearthed in the same area as some stone tools. The Leakeys concluded that *Homo habilis*, or "handy man," had been the first tool maker.

Mary's most important discovery came after the death of her husband. She and her team found a series of hominid footprints preserved in volcanic ash. Finding footprints might not seem very significant, but it gave the team an important piece of information. The footprints matched fossils found in the same area that were between 2.9 and 3.5 million years old. The footprints showed that the *Australopithecus afarensis*, an early ancestor of modern-day human beings, was able to walk upright.

Some of early human history is still a mystery to us today. Much of what we do know, though, is a result of the many years the Leakeys spent digging in the African dirt, searching for clues to our ancient past.

Circle the letter of the best answer to the question below.

1. Louis Leakey's belief that Africa was the "cradle of humanity" was

   a. supported by most of the scientific community of the 1920s.

   b. supported by the findings of ancient animal fossils.

   c. supported by the findings of human ancestors that were older than those found in Asia.

   d. not supported by any of the Leakeys' findings.

Write your answers on the lines below.

2. How did *Homo habilis* get its name?

   _____

3. Why were Louis and Mary a well-paired scientific team?

   _____

   _____

4. Using Louis Leakey as an example, explain how personality can play a role in one's success as a scientist.

   _____

   _____

5. Explain the importance of Mary Leakey's discovery of hominid footprints in volcanic ash.

   _____

   _____

6. How did Mary determine what kind of footprints she had found? Do you think this was a reliable method?

   _____

   _____

Unifying Concepts and Processes

Why do you think Louis was interested in helping to promote the study of primates?

_____

Vanishing Nature

extinct: no longer living or existing

salinity: degree of saltiness

invasive species: a species of plant or animal that is not native to an area; its introduction often causes changes to the existing populations of plants and animals

Species do not always remain on the list of extinct creatures forever. Occasionally, scientists will find new evidence of a plant or an animal that was thought for years to be extinct, such as the painted frog.

According to the Red List of Threatened Species, published by the World Conservation Union, nearly 16,000 species are currently threatened with extinction.

What causes plants and animals to become extinct?

When you think about species that have become **extinct**, you might picture dinosaurs or other prehistoric animals that are known only through fossil remains. It is not uncommon for plants and animals to have become extinct throughout Earth's history. However, the rates of extinction in the last 500 years may be 50 to 100 times their average rate throughout history.

A plant or animal is considered extinct when there has been a serious search for it over a period of time and no recent evidence can be found. By examining fossils, paleontologists have determined that there have been about five mass extinctions in history. Each one seems to be linked to changes in Earth's environment. For example, ice ages, changes in the **salinity** of Earth's oceans, and a change in sea levels have all been responsible for large numbers of species disappearing in a relatively short time. The largest extinction is believed to have taken place at the end of the Permian period, about 250 million years ago. Changes in sea level and ocean salinity caused the extinction of about 96 percent of marine animals and 77 percent of land animals.

During the last five centuries, human beings and human activity have been the main cause of rising rates of extinction. When land is cleared for development or for use in agriculture, animals lose their habitats and sometimes their lives. The pollution produced by industry, mining, and the burning of fossil fuels has also had a negative effect on plant and animal populations.

The greatest threat appears to have been the introduction of alien or **invasive species**. This can happen intentionally, as when a new crop is introduced to an area where it doesn't naturally grow. It can also happen accidentally, as when an animal or insect travels in a boat or plane's cargo from one side of the world to another. The round goby, for example, is a fish native to the Black and Caspian seas that was introduced into the Great Lakes though ships' ballast water.

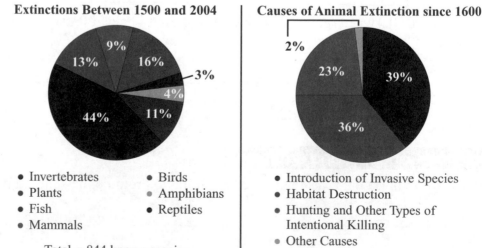

Extinctions Between 1500 and 2004

9% 16% 13% 3% 4% 44% 11%

- Invertebrates
- Plants
- Fish
- Mammals
- Birds
- Amphibians
- Reptiles

Total = 844 known species

Causes of Animal Extinction since 1600

2% 23% 39% 36%

- Introduction of Invasive Species
- Habitat Destruction
- Hunting and Other Types of Intentional Killing
- Other Causes

Using the charts, write **true** or **false** next to each statement below.

1. _____ Habitat destruction is the leading cause of animal extinction since 1600.

2. _____ To determine the number of mammals that have become extinct since 1500, you would find 9% of 844.

3. _____ Hunting is the cause of more than one-third of animal extinctions.

4. _____ Vertebrates and invertebrates have become extinct in nearly equal numbers.

Write your answers on the lines below.

5. How do scientists determine that a species has become extinct?

   _____

6. Give two examples of causes of mass extinctions in Earth's history.

   _____

7. Why might a plant or an animal be removed from the list of extinct organisms?

   _____

8. What method do scientists use to trace plant and animal extinctions through Earth's history?

   _____

9. The introduction of an invasive species can obviously present a threat to local species of plants and animals. Can you think of a time when introducing an alien species might benefit local plants or animals?

   _____

   _____

10. According to the pie chart, what category of organism has had the greatest number of extinctions? Why do you think this is?

   _____

   _____

What's Next?

Do some research online or at the library to learn more about species of plants and animals that are currently threatened with extinction. What is being done to protect them?

Lab Notes

solution: an equally distributed mixture of two or more substances

slurry ice: a mixture of ice, water, and salt that is used to cool substances below water's normal freezing point

Did the student use good scientific methods during this experiment?

Objective: I know that pure water freezes at 0°C, so I want to see how adding different substances to water changes the freezing point. I will measure the freezing point of pure water, water mixed with salt, water mixed with sugar, and water mixed with alcohol.

Hypothesis: The saltwater **solution** will have the lowest freezing point.

Details of the Experiment: First, I made my solutions. I poured one cup of water into Beaker 1 and set it aside. I poured one cup of water into Beaker 2 and then added one tablespoon of salt, stirring the solution until the salt was completely dissolved. I poured one cup of water into Beaker 3 and then added one tablespoon of sugar, again stirring the solution until the sugar was completely dissolved. I poured one cup of 40 percent isopropyl alcohol—the other 60 percent is pure water—into Beaker 4.

Next, I made a mixture of **slurry ice** in a large bowl by combining water, ice, and salt. I placed Beaker 1 into the slurry ice mixture and began stirring the pure water with a thermometer. I made sure the thermometer didn't touch the bottom of the beaker as I stirred. As soon as ice crystals began forming on the water in the beaker, I read the temperature on the thermometer and recorded the result. I repeated this procedure for the other three solutions.

Results: Freezing point of Beaker 1 (plain water): -0.5°C
Freezing point of Beaker 2 (saltwater solution): -4.5°C
Freezing point of Beaker 3 (sugar water solution): -4.5°C
Freezing point of Beaker 4 (40% isopropyl alcohol): -17.5°C

Conclusion: My hypothesis was not correct. A solution of alcohol and water will have the lowest freezing point.

Comments: I was surprised to see that both the sugar and salt solutions had the same freezing point. I also thought that alcohol, which is a liquid, would affect the freezing point less than a solid, like salt or sugar, would.

Circle the letter of the best answer to the question below.

1. What were the variables in this experiment?

    a. the solutions

    b. the freezing points

    c. the beakers

    d. the water

Write your answers on the lines below.

2. Write another hypothesis that could have been tested by this experiment.

    _____

3. Why was it important not to let the thermometer rest on the bottom of the beaker?

    _____

4. This student's experiment had an additional variable that made the conclusion unreliable. What was the additional variable, and how did it affect the experiment? [Hint: There are 16 tablespoons in a cup, so one tablespoon is 6.25 percent of one cup.]

    _____

    _____

5. Salt is often spread on roads during winter to prevent ice from forming. Do you think sugar would work as well? Explain your answer.

    _____

    _____

What's Next?

Do you think the boiling point of water would be affected in a similar way? Design an experiment similar to the one described in the selection, making sure you have an adult to help you. You'll also need to purchase or make a thermometer that attaches to the side of a container—you don't want to hold the thermometer in the boiling water! Heat each solution just until it begins to boil, and then record the temperature.

sterilized: rid or made free of living microorganisms

mortality rate: the number of deaths that occur in a group compared to the total number of members in that group

sepsis: an infection in the blood caused by high levels of bacteria

microorganisms: microscopic living creatures, such as bacteria

antiseptic: a substance that kills or prevents the growth of germs

Listerine® is a well-known brand of antiseptic mouthwash. It was named for Lister, in honor of his discovery of antiseptics.

At first, Lister believed that germs traveled through the air. He had a machine that sprayed a fine mist of carbolic acid into the operating room. It sterilized the entire room, but it could also irritate the skin and even the lungs of the doctors and nurses exposed to it repeatedly. Eventually, carbolic acid was replaced with milder boric acid.

What is the importance of having sterile conditions during medical procedures?

Imagine being prepped for surgery and finding out that your surgeon hadn't washed his or her hands. You'd probably be very concerned. Now, imagine that the tools the surgeon would use to perform the operation hadn't been **sterilized**. Would you let the surgery take place under conditions like these? Less than two centuries ago, this sort of scenario was common. It wasn't until British surgeon Joseph Lister questioned the accepted practices of the time that changes began to take place.

In the hospital where Lister worked, the **mortality rate** in one surgical ward was about 50 percent. After surviving their surgeries, the patients died as a result of what was called *hospital disease*. Today, it is better known as **sepsis**—an infection in the blood caused by **microorganisms**.

At the time, sepsis was thought to be caused by bad air, so the wounds were kept covered and protected after surgery. This just meant that the bacteria had a moist, dark home in which to grow and spread. Lister did his best to keep the operating rooms clean, but the mortality rates didn't change. He didn't believe that bad air was causing the infections. Instead, he thought that a very fine dust, similar to pollen, might be to blame. In a way, he was right, though he didn't know that this "dust" was actually alive.

In the 1860s, Lister read about the work of Louis Pasteur. He learned that Pasteur had found that microorganisms in living material can cause decay and disease. Lister decided to try using a chemical called *carbolic acid* to combat these microorganisms. It had been used to treat the strong odors of sewage, and Lister believed he might use it successfully in the operating room. He had surgeons wash their hands with it, cleaned the surgical tools with it, and treated wounds with it after surgery.

By 1869, in a space of just four years, the mortality rates dropped to about 12 percent in the same surgical ward where they had been nearly 50 percent. Lister had invented the first modern **antiseptic**, or sepsis-fighting solution.

Even though the results seemed obvious, many people were skeptical about Lister's methods and his ideas about germs. It wasn't until he successfully performed a new procedure under antiseptic conditions that other surgeons began to think that Lister's ideas might be valuable after all.

Write **true** or **false** next to each statement below.

1. _____ Surgeons around the world immediately accepted Lister's ideas about sterile conditions during surgery.

2. _____ During the first few years of using antiseptics, mortality rates changed very little.

3. _____ In the past, carbolic acid had been used to deodorize sewage.

4. _____ Carbolic acid causes bacteria to grow and spread.

5. _____ Before the mid-1860s, it was not common for doctors to wash their hands prior to surgery.

Write your answers on the lines below.

6. How did Lister use carbolic acid?

_____

_____

7. How was the work of other scientists important in Lister's discovery of antiseptics?

_____

8. What did Lister believe was causing sepsis? Why does the selection say that "in a way, he was right"?

_____

_____

9. What evidence did Lister have that the use of carbolic acid as an antiseptic was successful?

_____

What's Next?

The physicians Ignaz Semmelweis and Oliver Wendell Holmes also made important contributions in stopping the spread of germs and bacteria during medical procedures. Do some research to find out about their contributions and what others thought of their ideas at the time.

Older Than Time

dendrochronologist: a scientist who studies the rings of trees; from the Greek *dendros*, meaning "tree," and *chronos*, meaning "time"

increment borer: a tool that drills a hole and allows the user to extract the solid material through which the hole was drilled

Bristlecone pines can remain standing for hundreds of years after they die, instead of decaying or eroding. This has allowed scientists to use them to research changes in the climate over a period of thousands of years.

Bacteria have recently replaced trees as the oldest living organisms. Specimens have been found in a state of suspended animation, meaning scientists have been able to bring them back to life. One 25 to 40 million-year-old specimen was found in a bee preserved in amber. Other specimens have been found that are reported to be older, but these claims are not widely accepted.

What is the oldest living thing in the world?

Age is a relative thing. For an insect, two weeks might be a long life. For a human being, it might be 100 years. Trees are among the longest living organisms on the planet, and scientists have learned to determine their age with accuracy.

The most common method of dating trees is by counting the number of growth rings. In the spring, trees have a large burst of growth. It's followed by slower growth in the summer and little or no growth in the fall and winter. This cycle of growth produces one ring per year. By counting the layers or rings, scientists can determine the age of a tree.

A **dendrochronologist** can actually learn much more than just a tree's age by analyzing its rings. The colors and widths of the rings vary by year, depending on weather and other changes in climate. Droughts, rainy seasons, and heat waves are all recorded in the rings of a tree. Scientists can even learn about the effects of pollution by examining a tree's growth rings.

A nearly 5,000-year-old bristlecone pine, Methuselah, is the longest-living known tree today. By studying more than one ancient tree, scientists can extend their understanding of the climate over a long period of time. For example, when comparing the rings of a 3,000-year-old living tree with the rings of a nearby dead tree, they search for identical patterns of growth in the rings. If they find a match, this tells them when the dead tree was alive. Without a match, they can tell only how old it was when it died, not at what point during history it lived.

Using this method of overlap, scientists have been able to travel back about 8,000 years through history using the bristlecone pines of California's White Mountains. If scientists are able to go back 10,000 years, some very valuable information could be found. Many changes were taking place on Earth when the colder phase of the last ice age ended, so this period in history is particularly interesting for scientists.

It's easy to count growth rings in the cross-section of a tree. For living trees, though, this isn't possible. Instead, scientists use an **increment borer** to extract a long, thin sample of the tree without damaging it. The sample may be only a few millimeters in diameter, but it is still large enough to provide scientists with the information they need to explore history through the rings of a tree.

Circle the letter of the best answer to the question below.

1. An increment borer allows scientists to

   a. do a chemical analysis to determine a tree's precise age.

   b. extract material from a tree without cutting it down.

   c. date a tree by counting its growth rings.

   d. Both b and c

Write your answers on the lines below.

2. Explain how dead bristlecone pines are useful to scientists.

   _____

   _____

3. What kind of information can a dendrochronologist get from examining the rings of a tree?

   _____

   _____

4. Why do scientists hope to be able to add about 2,000 more years to the climate record they've created using bristlecone pines?

   _____

5. What is suspended animation?

   _____

Unifying Concepts and Processes

Some people don't think it's a good idea for scientists to bring ancient bacteria back to life. Explain why you think people might be worried about this. Do you think it is a valid concern?

   _____

   _____

What's Next?

Not all trees have growth rings. Find out how scientists measure the age of cycads, palm trees, and other trees that don't have rings.

Measuring the Stars

Sirius: one of the five closest stars to Earth, it's also the brightest star in the night sky

composition: the parts of objects and how they are put together

parallax: the apparent movement of an object when it is seen from two different points

geometry: a type of math that deals with lines, angles, and shapes

spectroscopy: using an instrument to create a spectrum of electromagnetic waves

Scientists can also measure a star's luminosity, or brightness. When this information is combined with a measurement of distance and temperature, a star's size can be determined.

How can scientists know how far away a star is?

The *Viking 2* spacecraft was launched 30 years ago and is just now reaching the outer edges of our solar system. It travels at more than 30,000 miles per hour, but even at that speed, nearly a million years will pass before it nears **Sirius**. The stars are incredibly far from Earth, but scientists have still managed to measure the distances and discover all sorts of information about the **composition** of the stars. How do they do it?

Let's start with distance. Hold your hand out in front of you, close one eye, and use your thumb to block out a small object on the far side of the room, like a light switch. Then, open the eye that was closed, and close the other eye. The object appears to move out from under your thumb and become visible again. This effect is called **parallax**. Scientists use parallax to measure how far away stars are.

When Earth is on one side of the sun, a careful observation is made of where a star is located in the sky compared to the other stars around it. Six months later, when Earth reaches the other side of the sun, the star is observed again. In the same way that the object you viewed appeared to move when you looked at it with one eye versus the other, the star appears to move a tiny bit in relation to some of the other stars.

Scientists then create a triangle using their measurements. The peak of the triangle is the star that is being measured. The base of the triangle is a straight line drawn from Earth when it's on one side of the sun to where it would be six months later on the other side. The way the star appears to move compared to the stars behind it—the parallax effect—creates the top angle of the triangle. Scientists can easily measure this angle. Then, they use **geometry** to calculate the length of the other two sides, which gives them the distance to the star.

A star's composition is found by using **spectroscopy**. When you shine sunlight through a prism, you see the different wavelengths of energy divided into a rainbow. In a similar way, spectroscopy separates the different wavelengths of energy emitted by stars. Each element emits a unique color when it's burned, so the different wavelengths of color that a star emits tell scientists which elements are burning inside it, as well as how hot it is.

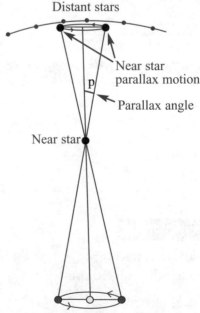

Distant stars

Near star parallax motion

p

Parallax angle

Near star

Earth's motion around Sun

Circle the letter of the best answer to each question below.

1. In the parallax example given in the selection, you used your thumb to block out a light switch. When scientists use parallax, which object from this example relates to the star that is being measured?

   a. your eyes

   b. your thumb

   c. the light switch

   d. None of the above

2. In order to calculate the distance to a star using parallax, an astronomer must know

   a. how far Earth travels in half a year.

   b. the distance from Earth to the sun.

   c. the distance from Earth to the nearest star.

   d. how far it is to the outer edge of our solar system.

3. This selection shows that astronomers can learn a lot about space by using

   a. experiments.

   b. telescopes.

   c. observation.

   d. solar radiation.

Write your answers on the lines below.

4. A spectroscope creates a spectrum, or array of colors, based on the light emitted by a star. How are scientists able to use these colors to determine which elements the star contains?

   _____

   _____

5. Why do you think luminosity, or brightness, alone isn't enough to tell you how far away a star is?

   _____

   _____

Changing with the Times

mollusks: invertebrate animals whose bodies are usually enclosed in a hard shell

evolved: developed a characteristic over time; usually results in a species having a better chance of survival

coexisted: lived together or nearby one another

When blue mussels thicken their shells, it's not an instant process. It usually takes place over a few months. The thickening uses up valuable energy, so the mussel does it only in response to the threat of crabs nearby.

When new traits evolve in a species, the process usually takes place over hundreds of years and many generations. Scientists have been able to trace the evolution of various species by looking at evidence of their development that appears in fossils.

Why does the recent evolution of mussels have scientists so amazed?

Blue mussels live in the Atlantic Ocean, off the east coast of the United States. Mussels are **mollusks**, and their shell protects them against many predators. Crabs, however, are able to crack the mussel's shell with their strong claws and get to the meat inside. Over a number of years, mussels have **evolved** a defense against certain species of crabs. Mussels can detect a chemical that crabs release. When a mussel determines that crabs are nearby, it thickens its shell. This makes it much harder for the crab to eat and may very well save the mussel's life.

Scientists have known about the relationship between crabs and mussels for years. The surprise came when two zoologists, Aaren Freeman and James Byers, observed something very interesting happening. In the late 1980s, an invasive species, the Asian shore crab, first entered U.S. waters. The crab arrived in the U.S. in ships, and, like other species of crabs, began feeding on blue mussels.

Freeman and Byers hypothesized that in a span of about 15 years, blue mussels evolved the ability to thicken their shells in defense against the Asian shore crab. How did the scientists know that this was a new response and not just the same defense the mussels already used?

Freeman and Byers decided to perform an experiment to test their hypothesis. They knew that Asian shore crabs didn't release the same chemicals as other crabs. They also knew that populations of the crabs had not yet reached northern Maine. If their hypothesis was correct, it would mean the Maine mussels would not thicken their shells when Asian shore crabs were nearby. They would not have detected the chemical in the water and would not yet know the crab was a predator.

The zoologists placed blue mussels from northern Maine in one bucket and blue mussels from elsewhere in New England in another bucket. When they added green crabs to the buckets, both sets of blue mussels thickened their shells. This made sense because both sets of mussels **coexisted** with green crabs. When they tried their experiment again using Asian shore crabs, the mussels from northern Maine did not thicken their shells. This meant that Freeman and Byers were correct—the blue mussels living in other parts of New England had evolved a defense mechanism in the short span of about 15 years.

Write **true** or **false** next to each statement below.

1. _____ In most species, evolution of a new trait takes place in less than ten years.

2. _____ Blue mussels thicken their shells as part of a mating ritual.

3. _____ Asian shore crabs release different chemicals than other species of crabs do.

4. _____ Thickening its shell is a defense mechanism of the Asian shore crab.

5. _____ Freeman and Byers used a combination of observation and experimentation in their investigation of blue mussels and Asian shore crabs.

Write your answers on the lines below.

6. Why is the Asian shore crab considered an invasive species in the United States?

_____

7. What was Freeman and Byers's hypothesis?

_____

8. Explain why both sets of mussels in the experiment thickened their shells in response to the green crabs but not to the Asian shore crabs.

_____

_____

_____

9. Why was it important to the experiment that blue mussels from northern Maine had never before been exposed to Asian shore crabs?

_____

_____

10. Why do you think Freeman and Byers's study was viewed as being important and was widely reported on?

_____

_____

Review

Circle the letter of the best answer to each question below.

1. Which of the following is not a step in the scientific method?

   a. designing an experiment

   b. doing research online

   c. drawing conclusions

   d. asking a question

2. Plants and animals are considered extinct when

   a. no signs of them have been found over a period of time.

   b. no fossils of them can be located.

   c. there are fewer than 10 existing individuals left of a species.

   d. Both a and b

3. Sterilizing materials used in surgery

   a. is no longer necessary in modern hospitals.

   b. is necessary only during outbreaks of certain viruses.

   c. combats infection caused by microorganisms.

   d. had no effect on the rates of sepsis in Joseph Lister's hospital.

Write **true** or **false** next to each statement below.

4. _____ Examining the hobbit's teeth allowed scientists to form a rough age estimate.

5. _____ Archaeologists study modern-day human life and cultures around the world.

6. _____ Footprints found by Mary Leakey proved early human beings couldn't walk upright.

7. _____ Rates of extinction have been much higher in the last 500 years than in the past.

8. _____ The only way to obtain a cross-section of a tree's trunk is by cutting it down.

9. _____ Blue mussels are considered an invasive species in the U.S.

10. _____ Spectroscopy allows scientists to determine the composition of stars.

Write your answers on the lines below.

11. Explain why language and communication are important skills for scientists to have.

_____

12. Give examples of two different scientific disciplines, and explain how observation plays an important role in each.

_____

_____

13. Why was the discovery of *Homo floresiensis*, considered so important in the scientific community?

_____

14. What does the use of fire and tools by a species indicate to scientists?

_____

15. Describe how human activity can contribute to the extinction of plants and animals.

_____

16. In the experiment that tested the freezing point of water, why were the student's results unreliable?

_____

17. Is a hypothesis that has been proven incorrect still useful? Explain.

_____

18. How did Joseph Lister use carbolic acid as an antiseptic? How did he know his efforts were successful?

_____

_____

19. What can a dendrochronolgist learn by examining the rings of a tree?

_____

20. Why was the study of blue mussels and their response to Asian shore crabs of great interest to scientists?

_____

Lesson 2.1   Everything Must Change

chemical reaction: a process that produces chemical change

One way to tell if chemical changes—and not just physical changes—are occurring is to watch for some of the following signs.

- The substance changes colors.
- Energy, in the form of heat or light, is emitted during the change.
- An additional gas or solid is produced.
- The change produces an odor.

Remember, matter and energy are never created or destroyed, they just change forms. When a chemical change occurs, all the atoms that formed the original substances still exist. They simply recombined to form new molecules in the new substances that the chemical reaction created.

What's the difference between a physical and a chemical change?

Matter changes all the time around you. Burn a log, and you end up with ash and smoke. An ice cube left in the sun melts into a pool of water. Drop a sugar cube into a glass of water, and it will slowly disappear.

The way matter changes can be either physical or chemical. Smash a glass jar and you still have glass. The matter is no longer jar-shaped, but it's still the same substance. That is a physical change. One way to determine if change is physical is to ask if the change can be reversed. For example, you can heat the broken pieces of glass until they turn to liquid, pour them into a jar-shaped mold, let it cool, and you'll have a jar again.

Physical changes often occur with increases or decreases in a substance's energy level. Remember, the three physical states of matter are solid, liquid, and gas. Matter is solid when it has the least amount of energy because its atoms and molecules are least active. As the energy level increases, the energized atoms and molecules need more room to bounce around, so the substance becomes less dense and changes from a solid to a liquid. More energy leads to more expansion, and the matter changes once again from a liquid to a gas.

Elements and substances can undergo this kind of physical change when enough energy is gained or lost. Water is a common example because we see it change states often—from solid ice to liquid water to gaseous steam. Solid metals like lead and iron undergo physical changes when they reach high enough temperatures and turn to liquid. As soon as they cool down, they become solid again.

When matter undergoes a physical change, it may look different, but at the molecular or atomic level it is still the same substance. A chemical change occurs when a substance changes into another kind of substance, and the change can't be reversed. For example, the ashes and smoke of a burnt log can't be put back together to form a piece of wood again.

Rust is another common example of a chemical change. Iron atoms exposed to air and water have a **chemical reaction** with oxygen. The atoms combine chemically to create a completely different substance—a molecule with three iron atoms and two oxygen atoms called *iron oxide*.

Circle the letter of the best answer to the question below.

1. In both physical and chemical changes,

   a. energy can be gained or lost.

   b. matter is created.

   c. matter is destroyed.

   d. Both a and b

Write your answers on the lines below.

2. What are three physical states of matter?

   _____   _____   _____

3. When atoms combine to form molecules, a _____ change has occurred.

Read each example of a change listed below. Decide whether the change was physical or chemical and explain how you know.

4. Fall arrives, and the leaves on the trees change colors.

   _____

5. Vinegar poured into baking soda produces a white, foaming substance that emits carbon dioxide.

   _____

6. Sugar is melted in a pan. It turns into a white liquid.

   _____

7. Sugar left on the stove too long starts to smoke and turns into a black solid.

   _____

8. A firework shot into the sky explodes into brilliant colors of light.

   _____

9. Hot asphalt poured onto flat ground cools to form a solid road surface.

   _____

10. Bread left in a bag in the dark turns green and has a strong odor.

    _____

A Common Reaction

oxidation: the process of combining chemically with oxygen

respiration: oxidation that occurs inside the cells of living organisms in order to create energy

acetic acid: the compound that gives vinegar its smell and taste

catalysts: substances that increase the speed of chemical reactions

Aluminum naturally protects itself from being destroyed by rust. A thin coating of aluminum oxide forms on the metal's surface due to oxidation. The layer prevents air and water from reaching the rest of the metal, though, so further oxidation doesn't occur.

Stainless steel—a mixture of iron, carbon, and chromium—forms a protective layer of chromium oxide due to oxidation.

Why is oxygen involved in so many chemical reactions?

Oxygen is the most abundant element in Earth's crust. It's also in the air we breathe and the water we drink. In fact, oxygen is Earth's most common element after iron, and it plays a role in many of the chemical reactions happening around—and even inside—you. Rotting fruit, rusting metal, and the carbon dioxide you exhale are all results of **oxidation**, which is oxygen molecules reacting with the molecules of other substances.

Fire is an example of very fast oxidation. When enough heat energy and oxygen molecules mix with the molecules in a fuel, they rapidly combine chemically to produce light, in the form of a flame, and heat.

Rust is an example of slow oxidation. Over time, oxygen molecules in air and water combine with iron atoms to form iron oxide molecules, better known as *rust*. Even though rust and fire are both forms of oxidation, you won't feel heat radiating from a rusting piece of metal because very little energy is involved in the reaction.

Respiration is oxidation happening inside the cells of plants and animals. Sugar and protein molecules in the cells react with oxygen and release the energy that your body needs to function.

Perform the following experiment to see oxidation in action. First, find an old copper penny. Then, get a plastic container with a lid that creates a tight seal. You'll also need some clay, a cotton ball, and vinegar.

Cover half of the copper penny with clay. Stretch the cotton ball, dip it into the vinegar, and then rub some vinegar onto the exposed copper. Place the vinegar-soaked cotton into the plastic container, and set the clay and copper on top of it. Seal the container with its lid.

After a few days, open the container. Remove the clay from the copper and you should see a difference between the two sides. The side that was covered by the clay will not have changed, but the side that was exposed to vinegar and oxygen should be darker and duller, and it might have even begun to turn green. This coloring is a layer of copper carbonate molecules formed through oxidation.

The copper will oxidize even if you don't use vinegar, but the process takes much longer. Vinegar contains **acetic acid**, and acids are **catalysts** that speed up the oxidation process.

Circle the letter of the best answer to each question below.

1. What is the most common element in Earth's crust?

   a. iron

   b. oxygen

   c. carbon

   d. aluminum

2. Which of the following is an example of oxidation?

   a. water evaporating

   b. sugar melting

   c. paper burning

   d. All of the above

Write your answers on the lines below.

3. Do you think the copper would have oxidized if it was completely submerged in vinegar? Why or why not?

   _____

   _____

4. Explain why stainless steel doesn't rust.

   _____

   _____

5. Why does acid rain damage monuments like the Statue of Liberty?

   _____

   _____

Unifying Concepts and Processes

When oxidation occurs, does a substance undergo a chemical change, a physical change, or both? Use a specific example of oxidation to explain your answer.

_____

_____

Testing the Waters

density: the quality of being made of matter that is packed closely together

mass: the quantity of matter something has

volume: the amount of space something takes up, measured in cubes

displaced: moved or shifted from one place to another

submerged: covered by or sunk below the surface of water

Ships made from iron or steel don't sink because of their shapes. The large volume of air contained by a boat's metal structure has very little weight, so a boat's overall density is less than water's. If enough water gets into a boat, though, the extra mass will increase the boat's density and cause the boat to sink.

How does density determine whether an object sinks or floats?

The students in Ms. Donahue's class began their experiment by calculating the **density** of water. First, they weighed an empty glass beaker. Then, they poured 0.5 liters of water into it and weighed it again. After subtracting the weight of the empty beaker, they saw that 0.5 liters of water weighs 500 grams, or 0.5 kilograms.

Density is found by dividing **mass** by **volume**, or $d = m/v$. The students used this formula to show that water's density is 1 kilogram per liter.

Next, the students filled a large, clear plastic tub with 20 liters of water and marked the water's level on the outside of the tub. Then, they placed a brick into the water. It quickly sank to the bottom and raised the water level. The students carefully removed the water the brick had **displaced** until the level returned to the original mark. The students measured the water they removed and found it had a volume of 960 milliliters, or 0.96 liters.

The students took the brick out of the water and weighed it. Its mass was 7 kilograms. They divided 7 by 0.96 to calculate the brick's density as 7.3 kilograms per liter.

Water was added to the tub to return the level to the 20-liter mark. A basketball was tested next. The students weighed the basketball first. It had a mass of 630 grams, or 0.63 kilograms. When the basketball was placed into the water, it floated, but it also displaced a small amount of water. As they had done before, the students removed water until the level matched the mark. Then, they measured the volume. They removed 630 milliliters, or 0.63 liters, of water.

They lifted the basketball out, added water back to the tub until it reached the mark, and then put the basketball back in. A student carefully pushed on the basketball until it was **submerged** just below the surface. Water was removed to reach the mark, and the volume was measured. The water removed this time had a volume of 7.1 liters.

Dividing 0.63 by 7.1 showed that the basketball's density was 0.09 kilograms per liter. The brick's density was much greater than water's density, while the basketball's was much less. The students concluded that an object denser than water sinks and displaces an amount of water equal to its volume. An object less dense than water floats and displaces an amount of water equal to its weight.

Circle the letter of the best answer to each question below.

1. The water displaced by the brick had a volume of 0.96 liters, which tells you that

   a. the brick's volume was 0.96 liters.

   b. the brick's volume was 9.6 liters.

   c. the brick's volume was 0.96 milliliters.

   d. the brick's weight was 960 milliliters.

2. A ship's total weight is equal to the weight of the water it displaces. If you want to calculate the ship's weight, you must first know

   a. the volume of water in the lake or ocean in which the ship is floating.

   b. the volume of the entire ship.

   c. the volume of the part of the ship that lies below the water's surface.

   d. All of the above

Write your answers on the lines below.

3. Why did the students need to weigh the glass beaker before they could calculate the weight of the water inside it?

   _____

4. How much did the water that was displaced by the brick weigh?

   _____

5. An object has a volume of 22 liters and a mass of 35 kilograms. What's the object's density? Will it float or sink in water?

   _____

What's Next?

Here's a simple experiment to test different shapes and their abilities to hold weight as they float. Cut several 12-inch x 12-inch squares of aluminum foil. Fold the squares into a variety of differently shaped containers. Some might have flat bottoms, while others are rounded. The sides can be taller, shorter, steeper, or flatter. Add pennies to each container until it sinks. Which containers carried the weight, and which ones didn't?

PLEASE DO NOT WRITE ON THE PAGES IN THIS BOOK. MAKE PHOTOCOPIES OF THE ONES YOU NEED.

Malleable Metals

conductivity: a substance's ability to carry an electrical current

ions: atoms that have a positive or negative electrical charge

reactive: takes part in a chemical reaction

malleable: able to be shaped or bent

Metals combine easily with other metals to form alloys. An alloy is a mixture of one metal with either another metal or a nonmetal. Alloys increase some characteristics of the original metal— usually strength. For example, steel, which is an alloy of iron and carbon, is much stronger than plain iron. Other examples of alloys are brass, which is a mixture of copper and zinc; bronze, which is a mixture of copper and tin; and pewter, which is tin, copper, and lead.

What makes a metallic element different from other elements?

When people describe metal, they usually use words like *hard*, *shiny*, and *solid*. Stomp on an aluminum soda can, though, and it easily crumples beneath your foot. Shine light at a chunk of lead, and the dull, dark surface absorbs most of it. Mercury, however, flows just like any other liquid. Even so, aluminum, lead, and mercury are all metals. In fact, nearly three-quarters of all the elements are considered metals. They aren't all exactly alike, but they do share a few traits.

The first is **conductivity**. The atoms of metallic elements easily lose electrons and become **ions** with positive charges. As you know, electricity is electrons on the move. Metals are good conductors because electrons flow quickly and easily among their atoms.

Metals are also **reactive**, especially with oxygen. Most metals that come into contact with water or air will oxidize, although some do it more quickly than others. Iron oxide, or rust, is the most familiar form of oxidation, but copper, aluminum, zinc, and nickel also have chemical reactions with oxygen over time. Drop sodium into water, though, and watch out. The oxidation is instant, resulting in an explosive release of energy.

The trait all metals share is the way their atoms are bonded together. At the molecular level, metals consist of positive ions held together by a swirling sea of shared electrons. Metallic atoms have strong bonds because they share all these electrons with each other. Metals are reactive because those electrons are readily available to bind with negative ions of other elements needing electrons. Electrons moving freely among the atoms are also why metals are such good conductors.

Sharing electrons makes metals **malleable**. You can easily bend, mold, or stretch a piece of heated metal without it breaking apart because metallic bonds are strong but not stiff. The atoms slide and stretch without pulling apart because the shared electrons slide and stretch with them.

Metals can be divided into several different categories. For example, the alkali metals, like sodium, potassium, and lithium, are extremely reactive. The transition metals are by far the largest category. Gold, silver, and copper are examples of transition metals.

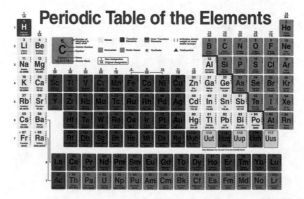

Periodic Table of the Elements

Circle the letter of the best answer to each question below.

1. Which of the following is not a metallic element?

    a. lithium

    b. nickel

    c. steel

    d. copper

2. What do conductivity and reactivity have in common?

    a. They both require electricity in order to happen.

    b. They both involve electrons.

    c. They both occur inside the nucleus of metallic atoms.

    d. Neither can occur in an alloy.

Write your answers on the lines below.

3. Why are metals good conductors?

    _____

    _____

4. How are alloys different than metallic elements?

    _____

    _____

5. Why do you think so many different products we use are made out of metal?

    _____

    _____

What's Next?

If three-quarters of the elements are metals, how are the remaining elements categorized? Look online or at the library for a copy of the periodic table of elements to find the answer.

A Force to Be Reckoned With

attractive force: strength or energy capable of pulling or attracting

exert: to put forth or to put into use

Newton's law also states that gravity between two objects is affected by distance. As the amount of space between two masses increases, the gravitational force they exert on each other weakens.

If gravity exists between Earth and the moon, why doesn't the moon crash into Earth? Imagine twirling a weight tied to the end of a string. The weight doesn't fly off through the air because the string holds it back and keeps it spinning around your hand. Similarly, the moon pulls away from Earth toward space, but gravity—the string— holds it in orbit around Earth.

What exactly is gravity?

Physicists don't know what gravity is. That sounds like an odd statement, but it's true. Now, you might think, *Drop a ball and it falls to the ground. That's gravity, right?* Knowing how gravity affects things, though, is very different from explaining why it happens.

What scientists do know about gravity begins around 1600 with the work of Galileo Galilei. His experiments showed that Earth's gravity pulls on all objects with the same amount of force. Whether an object is massive or tiny, it accelerates toward the ground at a single rate—32 feet per second squared. In other words, a bowling ball and a penny dropped from the same height will hit the ground at the same time. Weight has nothing to do with how quickly an object falls.

Then, later in the same century, Sir Isaac Newton published his Law of Universal Gravitation. He showed that gravity is an **attractive force** that exists between any two masses, regardless of their sizes. Two objects can have extremely different masses, but each exerts a gravitational force that pulls on the other. This means that any object on Earth—even something as small as a penny—has a gravitational force that pulls against the planet at the same time that the planet pulls against the object. Earth's mass is much larger, though, so it has a much stronger gravitational force. It always overwhelms the gravity you—or a bowling ball, penny, or bus—**exert**.

Newton's law also states that the total gravitational force can be found by multiplying the two objects' masses. This part of the law explains why you and a bus will fall to Earth at the same rate, even though the bus is much bigger than you are. Compared to Earth, you and the bus are hardly different at all. Multiply your mass with Earth's, and then compare it to the product you get by multiplying the bus's mass with Earth's. The difference is so small, it really doesn't matter—the total gravitational force is basically the same.

Something the size of the moon, though, has enough mass to affect Earth. As the moon orbits, its gravity pulls against the oceans as it passes over them. This causes the oceans to swell and brings high tides along the coasts. Once the moon moves along, and carries its gravitational force with it, the swelling stops and the tides recede.

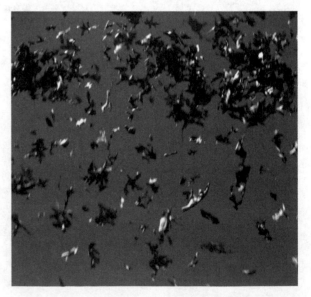

Circle the letter of the best answer to each question below.

1. Newton's Law of Universal Gravitation states that

    a. small masses don't exert gravity on larger masses.

    b. Earth's gravity cancels out the gravity that any other object might have.

    c. you exert a gravitational force against Earth.

    d. All of the above

2. Which object exerts a greater amount of gravitational force—a feather or a bowling ball?

    a. the feather

    b. the bowling ball

    c. They each exert the same amount of gravity.

    d. Neither of them has enough mass to exert any gravity.

Write your answers on the lines below.

3. Jupiter is much more massive than Earth. Would gravity be stronger or weaker there? Explain your answer.

    _____

    _____

Unifying Concepts and Processes

As Earth orbits the sun, each of them exerts a gravitational force on the other. Which object has the stronger gravitational force? How do you know?

_____

_____

What's Next?

Gravity is one of the four fundamental forces in the universe. Electromagnetism is another one. The other two are the strong force and the weak force that happen at the subatomic level. Find some information on what role these two forces play inside each atom and why one is considered strong and the other weak.

The Science of Vacuums

friction: a force that slows or resists motion when the surfaces of two substances come into contact

perfect vacuum: space that is empty of all matter and contains no gaseous pressure

gaseous pressure: the force created by the motion of a gas's atoms or molecules

The space inside an incandescent light bulb is a partial vacuum. Otherwise, the filament would quickly burn out if it came into contact with other gases.

One reason that perfect vacuums don't exist in nature is because the universe naturally moves toward entropy, or a state of equilibrium. In other words, areas with higher concentrations of matter always move toward areas of lower concentrations until matter is spread evenly throughout both areas. This is the second law of thermodynamics.

Is there such a thing as empty space?

Even if you remove everything from a room, it still won't be empty. The air is filled with atoms and molecules drifting about. Quickly wave your hand back and forth, and you'll feel a slight breeze. This sensation is caused by the **friction** of your hand moving past the particles. Before you have an absolutely empty space, you must remove all those atoms and molecules, too. Then, you'll have a **perfect vacuum**.

Perfect vacuums don't really exist anywhere in the universe, because there's no place completely free of matter. Even in space, there are still a few atoms and molecules floating around. These particles are spread far apart, so the amount of **gaseous pressure** they create is extremely low. One of the characteristics of a perfect vacuum is no gaseous pressure at all.

To understand this pressure better, think of gas molecules trapped inside a jar. As the molecules drift around, they bounce up against the sides of the container. Gaseous pressure is the force created by these molecules hitting the container. If you pump more molecules into the jar, the force of them hitting the glass increases. Keep pumping gas in, and eventually the pressure will increase beyond what the glass can handle, and the jar will shatter.

We live under the constant pressure of Earth's atmosphere. Miles and miles of gases weigh down on our bodies. We don't get crushed because the air inside our bodies exerts an equal amount of pressure outward, so the two pressures are equalized.

You can see the force of Earth's atmospheric pressure if you remove the air from inside a pop can. The can will quickly collapse because there is no longer any outward pressure to balance the inward pressure.

Atmospheric pressure is what keeps the molecules in liquids and gases on Earth from expanding indefinitely. In the low pressure of a vacuum, for example, water quickly evaporates and spreads evenly throughout the space. A balloon released in outer space would quickly pop for the same reason. With little gaseous pressure pushing against the balloon's exterior, the gas inside would expand and stretch the balloon until it burst.

Although perfect vacuums don't exist, scientists create partial vacuums by pumping the air out of jars or other containers. Then, they can perform experiments inside a space with almost no molecules—molecules that would otherwise create friction or cause unwanted chemical reactions.

Circle the letter of the best answer to each question below.

1. The moon has no atmosphere, so an astronaut's spacesuit must

   a. provide gaseous pressure.

   b. remove gaseous pressure.

   c. create gravity.

   d. Both a and c

2. A partial vacuum is created inside a jar. When the jar is opened

   a. air rushes out.

   b. air rushes in.

   c. the vacuum prevents air from moving into the jar.

   d. the vacuum increases and shatters the jar.

Write your answers on the lines below.

3. Why is a perfect vacuum impossible in nature?

   _____

   _____

4. Does water inside a vacuum boil at a higher or lower temperature than it does under normal pressures? Explain your answer.

   _____

   _____

5. Once spacecraft are launched from Earth, they need very little energy to cross vast distances. Why is this possible?

   _____

6. A scientist creates a nearly perfect vacuum in the lab. She places a cork inside. Does the cork float or lie at the bottom of the container? Explain your answer.

   _____

   _____

Sports Science

drag: a force that slows an object in motion by moving in the opposite direction

kinetic energy: the energy an object has because it's in motion; potential energy is the energy an object has because of its condition or position

inertia: Newton's first law of motion; see below

Newton's three laws of motion:

- First law of motion: An object in motion will remain in motion, and object at rest will remain at rest, unless acted on by another force. This is also known as *inertia*.

- Second law of motion: Force is mass times acceleration, written as F = ma. Remember, acceleration is how fast something speeds up.

- Third law of motion: For every action, there is an equal and opposite reaction.

How do physical forces affect sports?

Few people are more aware of forces than athletes. Sometimes, the forces they deal with are obvious. For example, a weight lifter competes against Earth's gravitational force. A swimmer fights through **drag** caused by the density of water. The ways in which forces affect some sports—and how the forces are overcome—are less obvious.

When a golfer swings a golf club, the solid wooden or metal head zooms toward the little white ball on the ground. Mathematically, force is defined as mass times acceleration, so the more quickly a golfer swings the club, the more force it will have.

Remember, a force is energy that can cause change. The golf club is loaded with **kinetic energy** as it moves around the golfer's body. When the club's head connects with the ball, this energy becomes a force that launches the ball through the air. As the golf ball soars, though, friction is created when it pushes past molecules in the air. Any part of a moving object's surface that contacts these molecules will create friction that slows it down. A golf ball is covered in dimples, or indentations, to minimize its surface area. Air molecules touch less of the ball's surface as it travels by them. With less drag, a ball will fly much farther.

When you hit a golf ball badly, it might skitter straight ahead through the grass. The dimples don't matter then. The ball's kinetic energy will be quickly used up as it runs into hundreds of blades of grass. Hit a hockey puck on ice with the same force, though, and it will sail smoothly many times farther.

The flat surface of a hockey puck sliding across slick ice creates little friction. Even if it's not traveling very quickly, a puck's **inertia** will carry it steadily along until another player knocks it in a different direction. Objects sliding on ice still create some friction, though, which becomes more obvious when you look at the players.

If hockey players slid around on flat-soled shoes, they wouldn't move anywhere near as far or as quickly as they do on skates. Like the dimples on a golf ball, the blade's thin edge means that very little surface area comes into contact with the ice. Skaters move smoothly and quickly because only a small amount of frictional force is created as the skate glides across the ice.

Circle the letter of the best answer to each question below.

1. Which of these objects has the most force when it's accelerating at 20 feet per second squared?

   a. a bowling ball rolling down the lane

   b. a baseball flying through the air

   c. a hockey puck sliding across ice

   d. a soccer ball rolling across the field

2. Hockey Player A weighs much more than Player B. If both players are pushed from behind with equal forces, Player A will come to a stop first because of

   a. gravity.

   b. friction.

   c. inertia.

   d. Both a and b

Write your answers on the lines below.

3. A baseball and a bowling ball are thrown in the same direction and have the same acceleration. The bowling ball had to be launched with more force, but it traveled the same distance as the baseball before hitting the ground. Why?

   _____

4. Describe how gravity, inertia, and friction play a role in throwing a ball.

   _____

   _____

   _____

Unifying Concepts and Processes

A pole-vaulter runs down a track, plants one end of the pole into the ground, and then jumps in the air while bending the pole. As the pole unbends, it creates a force that launches the pole-vaulter up and over the bar. Using your knowledge of potential and kinetic energy, describe how the pole is like a spring.

_____

_____

_____

The Spectrum: The Long and the Short of It

electromagnetic radiation: waves of energy that contain both electric and magnetic properties

spectrum: the range of electromagnetic waves, from long sound waves to short gamma rays

wavelengths: the distances measured from the peak of one wave to the peak of the next wave

frequencies: measurements of how many waves pass a fixed point in a set amount of time

range: a sequence or series with a set beginning and ending

The electromagnetic waves of energy in the spectrum can be discussed in terms of wavelength, frequency, or energy level. These three things are different, but they're closely related. Just remember that the longest wavelengths have the lowest frequencies and least amount of energy. The shortest wavelengths have high frequencies and the most energy.

The ozone layer filters out a lot of the sun's ultraviolet radiation, but some of it still reaches Earth's surface.

What is electromagnetic energy?

Electromagnetic radiation travels through the universe as waves of energy. Sometimes, you feel these waves as heat, and sometimes you see them as light. They can carry information across space as radio waves, or they can pass through bodies to make X-rays.

The electromagnetic **spectrum** lists these waves in order of their **wavelengths**. It begins with the longest wavelengths, which also have the lowest **frequencies** and contain the least amount of energy. It ends with the shortest wavelengths. They have a lot of energy and high frequencies.

Sound waves are the longest waves and contain very little energy, although you can certainly feel them at times. The pounding bass of a loud stereo will noticeably bounce sound waves against your body. As sound waves get shorter, they produce higher sounds, and beyond a certain point, human ears can no longer detect them.

Radio waves come next in the spectrum. Cell phones, televisions, radios, and wireless computers all use radio waves to send and receive coded messages. Radio waves don't contain much energy, so having them bounce around in Earth's atmosphere doesn't pose much danger.

The shortest radio waves are microwaves. They contain enough electromagnetic energy to have a noticeable effect on matter. Microwave ovens use this energy to excite the atoms and molecules in food and heat it.

The next section of the spectrum is infrared light. These waves are too long to see, but they have enough energy to make your skin feel warm. They come right before visible light on the spectrum. Visible light is the **range** of electromagnetic frequencies that human beings can detect with the cells in their eyes. We see color depending on which wavelengths of visible light— red, orange, yellow, green, blue, indigo, or violet—are reflected or absorbed.

After visible light, the wavelengths in the spectrum continue to get shorter, more energetic, and more dangerous. Just beyond the range of human sight is ultraviolet light. You can't see it, but if you spend time in the sun, you'll know it was there because of your sunburn.

At the top of the spectrum are X-rays and gamma rays. Radioactive materials emit these short, energetic wavelengths. This form of radiation is the most dangerous because it can pass right into cells and damage them.

Radio	Microwaves	Infrared	Visible	Ultraviolet	X-ray	Gamma Ray

Low Frequency   High Frequency

Long Wavelength   Short Wavelength

NAME _____

Circle the letter of the best answer to each question below.

1. What is the electromagnetic spectrum?

   a. a system used to measure radiation

   b. the range of the different wavelengths of radiation

   c. a list of electromagnetic energy forms that human beings can't detect

   d. All of the above

2. Microwaves are

   a. a type of radio wave.

   b. longer than visible light waves.

   c. shorter than gamma rays.

   d. Both a and b

3. Which forms of electromagnetic energy pose the greatest danger to human beings?

   a. radiation with longer wavelengths than radio waves

   b. microwaves and infrared light

   c. radiation with shorter wavelengths than visible light

   d. radiation with longer wavelengths than ultraviolet light

Write your answer on the lines below.

4. Are the light waves reflecting off a red stop sign longer or shorter than the waves reflecting off a violet-colored jacket? Explain how you know.

   _____

   _____

Unifying Concepts and Processes

Like gravity, electromagnetic energy is considered one of the four fundamental forces. Review the definition of *force*. Then, give a specific example of electromagnetic energy as a force.

_____

The Smallest of the Small

particles: very small pieces or parts of matter

physicists: scientists who study physics, or the science of matter and energy

fission: splitting an atom's nucleus

model: a description or construction that helps explain something that can't be easily understood or seen

The word *quark* originally comes from a nonsense word used in a line from James Joyce's novel *Finnegan's Wake:* "Three quarks for Muster Mark!"

Physicists have also discovered that particles of matter can have exact opposites, called *antimatter.* Antimatter can't be seen, but evidence of it appears during many subatomic experiments. When a particle comes into contact with its corresponding antiparticle, the two pieces of matter often destroy each other. Lucky for us, the universe contains a lot more matter than it does antimatter!

Every proton and neutron is made up of three quarks.

What in the world are quarks and leptons?

Organisms are made of cells. Cells are made of molecules. Molecules are made of atoms. Atoms are made of electrons, protons, and neutrons. But does it end there?

By the early part of the 1930s, three subatomic **particles** had been discovered and proven to exist. Scientists knew that protons and neutrons huddled together inside an atom's nucleus, and much tinier electrons buzzed around outside it. However, as **physicists** continued experimenting with radioactive decay and **fission**, they kept finding new particles that definitely weren't protons, neutrons, or electrons.

Dozens of these particles had been found by the time the 1960s began. Neutrinos, muons, pions, mesons, leptons, and deltas are just a few of their names. The original idea that everything in the universe was made of just protons, neutrons, and electrons no longer made sense. A new **model** of the universe's structure needed to be found.

In 1964, physicists Murray Gell-Mann and George Zweig introduced the Quark Theory of particles. Their theory said that all the different subatomic particles that had been discovered were simply different combinations of just two types of even tinier particles—quarks and leptons. By the 1970s, the Standard Model had developed based on the research of many scientists. It successfully explained almost everything occurring at the subatomic level.

Quarks come in six different "flavors"—up, down, top, bottom, charm, and strange. Lone quarks are never found in nature. They always exist in pairs or trios, and it's these combinations of quarks that form nearly all the other types of particles.

The only particles of matter that aren't made up of quarks are leptons. The best known type of lepton is the electron. Two others—the tau lepton and the muon lepton—are about the same size as electrons, but they're extremely rare particles in nature. Almost as soon as tau and muon leptons come into existence, these unstable particles break apart to form two quarks and one of nature's tiniest bits of matter—a lepton called a *neutrino*.

Like neutrons, neutrinos have no electrical charge. Although the universe is filled with them, neutrinos are so small that they usually pass right through Earth's atoms without coming into contact with other particles.

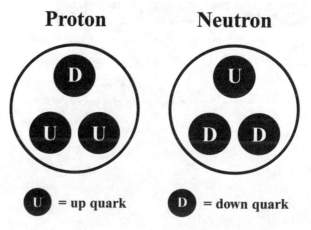

Proton   **Neutron**

U = up quark   D = down quark

Circle the letter of the best answer to each question below.

1. Which of the following are not types of quarks?

   a. left and right

   b. up and down

   c. charm and strange

   d. top and bottom

2. Quarks are always found

   a. alone in nature.

   b. inside electrons.

   c. in pairs or trios.

   d. with leptons.

3. Protons and neutrons are made of

   a. a pair of leptons.

   b. three quarks each.

   c. several different electrons.

   d. muons and taus.

4. Why are tau and muon leptons so rare?

   a. They are extremely unstable.

   b. They are quickly destroyed by neutrinos that crash into them.

   c. Scientists have no idea how to create them in the lab.

   d. All of the above

Write your answer on the line below.

5. Why did Murray Gell-Mann, George Zweig, and other scientists need to develop the Standard Model?

_____

What's Next?

This selection is only a brief introduction to the subatomic world of quarks and leptons. For example, why are some quarks strange and others charmed? Why must they always combine in twos or threes? How in the world did physicists discover something as tiny as a neutrino? Do some research to find out.

NAME _____

Circle the letter of the best answer to each question below.

1. Which of the following is not a common sign that a chemical change has occurred?

   a. A substance changes in color.

   b. An odor is produced.

   c. A substance changes states from solid to liquid.

   d. Light is produced.

2. Respiration is a form of oxidation that

   a. occurs in cells.

   b. produces fire.

   c. causes rust.

   d. creates oxygen.

3. Water molecules inside a vacuum will

   a. become densely packed together.

   b. expand and spread evenly throughout the space.

   c. form ice because there's no heat energy in a vacuum.

   d. be drawn to the bottom of the container because of gravity.

4. Which of the following subatomic particles have the least amount of mass?

   a. quarks

   b. protons

   c. neutrinos

   d. electrons

Write your answers on the lines below.

5. An object that floats will displace its _____ in water, while an object that sinks

   will displace its _____ in water.

6. Why are metals good conductors?_____

7. Why would a grain of sand and a piano fall to the ground at the same rate when dropped from the same height?

   _____

NAME _____

8. Give one specific example each of a physical change and a chemical change.

_____

9. Oxidation is a _____ change that involves oxygen and other matter.

10. When aluminum is exposed to air and water, a thin layer of aluminum oxide forms on the surface. Why is this oxidation helpful?

_____

11. Choose a sport, and then describe how friction, gravity, and inertia affect the action.

_____

_____

12. List these forms of electromagnetic energy in order from longest to shortest wavelength: microwaves, ultraviolet light, gamma rays, radio waves, sound, X-rays, visible light.

_____

Use the words in the box to complete the sentences below.

reaction	gaseous	drag	gravity	electromagnetic
malleable	dense	alloy	catalyst	

13. _____ is an attractive force that exists between any two pieces of matter.

14. Acid acts as a _____ to increase the speed of oxidation.

15. Rust is a chemical _____ that involves iron and oxygen.

16. Stainless steel is an iron, carbon, and chromium _____ that doesn't rust.

17. Whether an object floats or sinks is determined by how _____ it is.

18. Metals are _____ because their atoms have strong but flexible bonds.

19. Air inside our bodies exerts _____ pressure that balances the pressure created by Earth's atmosphere.

20. Airplanes in flight have to overcome _____ created by gases in the atmosphere.

21. The shortest wavelengths of _____ energy are the most dangerous.

Lesson 3.1   Anatomy of a Cell

organelles: structures inside a cell that perform specific functions

chromosomes: long molecules of DNA, containing the genetic information of the cell

protein: a long chain of amino acid molecules that plays an essential role in all life

enzymes: special proteins produced by cells; they help speed up chemical reactions

Animal cells and plant cells are similar, but there are two important differences. First, a plant cell membrane is surrounded by an additional cell wall that helps protect it and gives the cell a rigid structure. Plant cells also contain chloroplasts, which are special organelles that allow photosynthesis to occur.

How does a cell change food into energy?

Eating, drinking, and breathing bring chemicals from the surrounding environment into your body. Systems in your body transport these chemicals to where they're needed, but it's your cells that make them useful.

In a way, each cell is like an individual, living organism. It uses oxygen, digests food, makes waste, and reproduces. Like the organs in your body, cells contain **organelles** that help them function. Here's a brief overview of cell anatomy.

- The cell membrane is a cell's outer skin. It controls which molecules enter or exit the cell. Inside the membrane, a cell is filled with a clear fluid called *cytoplasm*, where the organelles are found.

- The largest organelle is the nucleus. It controls most of the cell's activities, and it's home to DNA molecules called **chromosomes**. Inside the nucleus is the nucleolus, where parts of the ribosome are formed.

- Ribosomes are the cell's **protein**-making machines. Proteins do most of the work in the cell, as building blocks of the organelles or as **enzymes**.

- The endoplasmic reticulum, or ER, is attached to the outside of the nucleus. Ribosomes sit on the ER, where they make proteins. The ER packages the proteins inside organelles called *vesicles*, which float through the cytoplasm to reach the Golgi body.

- The Golgi body does the final processing of proteins. It repackages the proteins that came from the ER into vesicles that are then returned to the cytoplasm.

- Lysosomes are special vesicles that make this trip from the ER, to the Golgi body, and back out into the cytoplasm. They begin as simple chemicals in the ER, but are turned into complex enzymes. Then, the Golgi body packages the enzymes into a vesicle called a *lysosome*. Lysosomes help break down sugars and proteins.

- The biggest source of energy inside a cell is the mitochondria. Respiration occurs inside these organelles. Remember, respiration is a form of oxidation— oxygen combines with food molecules and releases energy. Enzymes are catalysts that increase the speed of the chemical reactions.

- Vacuoles are organelles that move waste and harmful chemicals to the cell membrane so they can be removed.

Circle the letter of the best answer to each question below.

1. What do the endoplasmic reticulum and Golgi body have in common?

   a. They both transform food molecules into energy.

   b. They both play a role in cell division.

   c. They both create vesicles.

   d. They're both attached to the nucleus.

2. Proteins are created by

   a. the cytoplasm.

   b. the lysosomes.

   c. the ribosomes.

   d. the mitosis.

3. Which part of a cell is not found in the cytoplasm?

   a. chromosomes

   b. Golgi body

   c. ribosome

   d. vacuole

Write your answer on the lines below.

4. What do mitochondria do inside the cell?

   _____

   _____

Unifying Concepts and Processes

In the selection about oxidation, vinegar was used as part of an experiment to change the appearance of copper. In this selection, you learned that oxygen, food molecules, and enzymes are all part of respiration. Which of these three chemicals plays the same role in oxidation as vinegar did in the experiment? Explain your answer in detail.

   _____

   _____

   _____

Homeostasis: The Balance of Life

systems: groups of objects or entities that work together for a common goal

dilate: grow wider or larger

constrict: grow narrower or smaller

diffusion: atoms or molecules moving from areas of higher concentration to areas of lower concentration

equilibrium: a stable, balanced system where equal forces oppose each other

Warm-blooded animals maintain a steady body temperature because of how their bodies react to changing external temperatures. Cold-blooded animals don't have this same self-regulating ability. In order for them to keep their body temperatures regulated, they have to find an external source of heat, like a warm place in the sun.

Homeostasis plays a role in larger living systems as well. For example, if an animal is removed from an ecosystem, all the other organisms will be affected as the ecosystem attempts to return to a balanced state.

Why do you stop feeling hungry after you've eaten a meal?

Living organisms are carefully controlled **systems**. If one part doesn't work properly, the entire system can become unstable, and the organism will get sick or even die. The word *homeostasis* means "proper balance." The proper balance of chemicals and heat allow the organisms to stay healthy.

In human beings and other mammals, a region of the brain called the *hypothalamus* plays a big role in homeostasis. For example, it regulates the amount of heat in your blood and helps you maintain a stable internal body temperature. If your blood is too warm, the hypothalamus sends signals through the nervous system to your sweat glands and blood vessels. Sweat evaporates from your skin and carries heat away from your body. The blood vessels near your skin's surface also **dilate**, which brings more blood near the outside of your body where the heat can more easily exit.

When you get cold, these blood vessels **constrict** so that blood stays away from your skin's surface, and you don't lose as much heat. You also begin shivering. The quick, repetitive contraction of your muscle cells burns fuel and creates heat at the cellular level that helps warm your blood. The hypothalamus doesn't just regulate heat, though. It also tells you when you're thirsty, hungry, or sleepy.

All the chemical processes that keep an organism alive occur at the cellular level, and maintaining homeostasis is equally important there. Cell membranes regulate the molecules that enter or exit the cell through a process called **diffusion**.

In nature, a high concentration of matter will always flow toward a low concentration until there is **equilibrium**. For example, air molecules inside a balloon are highly concentrated. Untie the balloon, and the molecules rush out into the lower concentration of molecules in the outside air until they are spread evenly through both spaces. This process is diffusion.

Molecules of water, oxygen, carbon dioxide, and other chemicals are found both inside and outside a cell. A cell can't function properly if there are too few or too many of these molecules inside it. When the water inside a cell becomes highly concentrated with carbon dioxide, the CO_2 molecules pass through the cell membrane and spread through the surrounding fluids until the concentration of CO_2 inside and outside the cell are equal. In the same way, higher concentrations of oxygen outside the cell will cause oxygen molecules to pass into the cell until equilibrium is reached.

warm-blooded mammal   **cold-blooded reptile**

Circle the letter of the best answer to each question below.

1. Which of the following is not an example of diffusion?

   a. a drop of food coloring spreading through a glass of water

   b. perfume filling a room

   c. salt spilled onto a table

   d. air leaking from a tire

2. Which of these actions isn't part of your body's homeostasis?

   a. sweating when you are hot

   b. breathing harder when you exercise

   c. smiling when you're happy

   d. going to the bathroom

Write your answers on the lines below.

3. Use homeostasis to explain why you might throw up if you eat food that has gone bad.

   _____

4. Do you think a cell ever reaches a state of equilibrium? Explain your answer.

   _____

5. What would happen if your hypothalamus didn't work properly?

   _____

   _____

Unifying Concepts and Processes

Review the definition of *entropy* on page 36 and use it to explain why diffusion occurs.

_____

_____

What's Next?

James Lovelock's Gaia Hypothesis states that Earth is a giant living organism because, like every other living organism, it is a natural system controlled by homeostasis. Do some research to learn more about the Gaia Hypothesis.

traits: the qualities or characteristics that a person has

heredity: biological characteristics passed from parent to child through genes

geneticists: scientists who study genetics, or the science of heredity

dominant: having the most influence or control

Based on his research, Galton developed an idea called *eugenics* that suggested only healthy, intelligent people should be allowed to have children. For several decades, many prominent scientists and political leaders agreed with Galton and saw eugenics as a great way to improve the human race. Eventually, these ideas were used in Nazi Germany to justify the mass murders of millions of people. Scientists saw the danger in this kind of thinking, and today eugenics is seen by most people as an unethical and immoral idea.

Do genes determine your destiny?

The genes in your DNA determine physical **traits**. Genes determine hair texture, eye color, height, and all the other things that make up your appearance. There's no debate that genes are the building blocks of your body, but where do your likes and dislikes come from? Do genes cause a person to become an athlete, love broccoli, or enjoy opera? Since the mid-1800s, scientists have examined the question of whether **heredity** or the environment in which you are raised is more important in forming who you are—a debate known as "nature versus nurture."

This phrase was popularized by Francis Galton in 1865. Galton believed that inherited traits are the most important factor in creating our personalities. His research found that the intelligent men he knew also happened to have intelligent fathers. Intelligence seemed to pass directly through the generations—from grandfather to father to son, for example—but was less common between cousins. Other scientists argued that the intelligence Galton saw was due to environment, and it had nothing to do with genetically inherited traits.

During the 20th century, scientists eagerly investigated how environmental factors, such as education and family life, combined with genetics to influence our personalities. Although a definitive answer still hasn't been found, scientists agree that the best research into the nature versus nurture debate focuses on twins and adopted children.

Fraternal twins are no more alike than any other pair of siblings, but identical twins share the exact same genetic make-up. This characteristic gives psychologists and **geneticists** two genetically identical people to compare. As the twins' personality traits develop over time, scientists take note of which environmental factors were different between the two siblings. Researchers are especially fascinated by identical twins who were raised in separate households due to adoption and then later reunited. These twins often show surprising similarities in their likes and dislikes.

Science may never completely prove whether nature or nurture plays a more **dominant** role in making us who we are. It's clear, though, that our genes, families, and friends are all part of it. A great athlete may inherit physical traits, but without encouragement from a coach and hours of practice, his or her talents would never reach their full potential.

Circle the letter of the best answer to each question below.

1. Physical traits pass from one generation to the next

   a. through genes.

   b. because of environment.

   c. according to eugenics.

   d. All of the above

2. "Nature versus nurture" can also be described as

   a. "heredity versus genetics."

   b. "DNA versus inheritance."

   c. "genes versus environment."

   d. "dominant versus submissive."

3. Which physical trait is most likely to be influenced at least partly by environment?

   a. height

   b. hair color

   c. weight

   d. eye color

Write your answers on the lines below.

4. A mother and daughter are both talented pianists. Give an inherited trait and a learned trait that would lead to this similarity.

   _____

   _____

5. How do identical twins differ from fraternal twins?

   _____

6. Why would an adopted child be a good candidate for a study of nature versus nurture?

   _____

   _____

The Ankle Bone's Connected to the Leg Bone

buffered: protected from harm

sac: a small bag that usually contains fluid

mobile: able to be moved

inflammation: the body's response to injury or infection; includes swelling and pain

Ligaments stretch across the joints from bone to bone. If you are "double jointed," you don't have extra joints, but you can bend them farther than most people.

At the base of the thumbs are saddle joints that allow your thumbs to touch your other fingers. These are the only saddle joints in your body.

While it is usually older people who suffer from arthritis, juvenile rheumatoid arthritis affects children. No one knows exactly what causes it, but research has shown that it affects the immune system—the body's system of fighting bacteria and viruses.

How do joints help your body move?

A basketball star dribbles down the court and bounds into the air for a slam dunk. A figure skater glides across the ice, leaps, and lands a triple flip-triple loop combination jump. What these athletes have in common is that they rely on the interaction of their bones, joints, and muscles.

You know that your bones provide a framework for your body and muscles power the motion, but what are joints? Joints—the points where two bones meet—keep bones in alignment and allow your skeleton to move.

The three main types of joints are classified by the amount of movement they allow. Fibrous joints do not permit any movement. Instead of being formed by a single large bone, the skull is made of bony plates that fit together like a puzzle. In between the plates is connective tissue, which is a fibrous joint.

Cartilaginous joints move just a little. The two bones that meet at a joint are **buffered** by a disc of a smooth, slightly soft substance called *cartilage*. The spine is comprised of a stack of 33 bones called *vertebrae* with 23 layers of cartilage in between. The cartilaginous joints between the vertebrae are what enable the back to bend. The bottom nine vertebrae lack cartilage and are fused in two groups to form the tailbone and the pelvis.

Synovial joints are able to move in many directions. In these joints, the ends of the bones are covered with cartilage. A **sac** of fluid surrounds the joint to provide lubrication. Three main types of synovial joints play a major role in voluntary movement. Hinge joints allow back-and-forth movement, which is similar to opening and closing a door. Elbows, knees, and fingers all have hinge joints. Pivot joints let you rotate your head. Ball-and-socket joints in the shoulders and hips are the most **mobile** joints, permitting a circular movement. In fact, the shoulder is the most flexible joint in the human body, allowing you to swing your arms in any direction.

When joints are working properly, we don't give them much thought. One problem they can develop, though, is a disease called *arthritis*. In some types of arthritis, old age and previous injuries can wear down the cartilage and cause the bones to rub against each other. This creates **inflammation** near the joint, and sufferers develop severe pain, stiffness, and exhaustion. Exercising regularly and eating a nutritious diet can help you avoid some painful joint problems and keep your body moving smoothly.

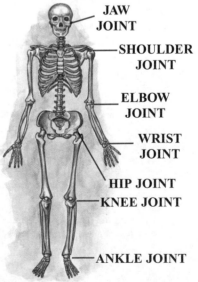

JAW JOINT

SHOULDER JOINT

ELBOW JOINT

WRIST JOINT

HIP JOINT

KNEE JOINT

ANKLE JOINT

Use the words in the box to complete the sentences below.

inflamed	ligaments	fibrous	circular

1. _____ joints, like those in your skull, do not allow any movement.

2. When a part of the body becomes injured, it may become _____.

3. A person who is double jointed has longer _____ than most people.

4. Ball-and-socket joints allow _____ movement.

Write **true** or **false** next to each statement below.

5. _____ Arthritis affects only people who are middle-aged or older.

6. _____ Saddle joints are found only in the thumbs.

7. _____ The knee joint is the most flexible joint in the human body.

8. _____ Cartilaginous joints allow less movement than synovial joints.

Write your answers on the lines below.

9. What is the purpose of joints in the human body?

_____

10. How is a ball-and-socket joint different from a hinge joint? Give one example of each.

_____

_____

11. Explain why part of the spine bends and part of it does not.

_____

12. What purpose does cartilage serve? What happens when it wears down?

_____

_____

13. Why would joint health be important to an athlete?

_____

Antibiotics: Life Killing Life

compounds: two or more substances that have combined together chemically to form a new substance

exuded: oozed out gradually, as in sweat or droplets

synthetic: produced artificially

strain: a subgroup of organisms that have unique characteristics but aren't classified as a new species

Modern researchers weren't actually the first people to understand the importance of antibiotics. The Chinese used antibiotics more than 2,500 years ago. The ancient Egyptians used a mixture of lard, honey, and lint as an ointment for treating wounds. The honey contained antibacterial properties and acted as a disinfectant. The ancient Greeks used mold to treat cuts and scrapes.

Not all bacteria are harmful to the body. Probiotics are "good" bacteria found in dietary supplements or in foods like yogurt. These bacteria are naturally found in your body and can help with digestion and boost your immune system.

Where do antibiotics come from, and how do they work?

Have you ever been ill and taken antibiotics? Antibiotics are chemical **compounds** that help the body fight infection by destroying or inhibiting the growth of microorganisms like bacteria.

Modern antibiotics were discovered in France in 1897 by Ernest Duchesne, a young physician, when he found that a certain type of mold called *Penicillium* would heal wounds. He was ignored because of his youth, and his research went largely unnoticed.

In 1928, Scottish biologist Alexander Fleming rediscovered the antibiotic properties of *Penicillium*. While Fleming was studying a bacterium, he carelessly allowed some mold to grow in his petri dishes along with the bacteria. Returning from a vacation, Fleming observed that the mold **exuded** a liquid substance that killed the bacteria. Fleming named his discovery *penicillin*, but never was able to develop it for practical uses.

Ten years later, Ernst Chain and Howard Florey expanded on Fleming's work. They created a purified form of penicillin and used it to treat mice that had been infected with lethal doses of bacteria. During World War II, the team of scientists quickly applied their findings to human patients. They worked with the government to establish factories to mass produce the drug and used penicillin to save the lives of millions of soldiers. Penicillin is still one of the most widely prescribed antibiotics.

There are approximately 100 antibiotics in use today, and researchers continue to hunt for new forms. Some antibiotics are **synthetic** and are manufactured by scientists in laboratories. Others have natural sources—one of the many reasons that preserving the world's rain forests is so important. Plants found in these areas are used to make lifesaving drugs.

It is important that physicians prescribe antibiotics only when they are necessary. Antibiotic treatment may not kill every single bacterium. The bacteria that survive are resistant to that drug. Because only these resistant bacteria can survive and reproduce, a drug-resistant **strain** is created. When an antibiotic is used more frequently, drug resistance becomes more likely. Eventually, antibiotics that could once be used to cure illnesses become less effective and alternatives have to be found. Scientists must constantly search for ways to combat newer, antibiotic-resistant strains of bacteria in order to keep some of the world's most dangerous diseases under control.

Write **true** or **false** next to each statement below.

1. _____ All bacteria are harmful to the body.

2. _____ When antibiotics are used too frequently, they can become ineffective.

3. _____ Penicillin was the first modern antibiotic to be widely used.

4. _____ All antibiotics are obtained from natural sources, such as mold.

Write your answers on the lines below.

5. Explain how the modern discovery of antibiotics required scientists to build on the work of others in the field.

   _____

   _____

6. In recent years, antibacterial hand soaps have become very popular. Do you think the widespread-use of these soaps is wise? Explain your answer.

   _____

   _____

7. One problem with using pesticides to control insects on crops is that the insects can develop resistance to the chemicals. How is this similar to the overuse of antibiotics?

   _____

   _____

8. Give one example of how a group of ancient people used a version of antibiotics.

   _____

9. Why do you think there was a rush to mass produce penicillin around the time of World War II?

   _____

10. What are probiotics, and how are they used?

   _____

Nature's Talented Weavers

spinneret: a spider's organ that produces silk thread

radials: the spokes that extend from the center of a circular shape, such as a spider's web or a wheel

Trap-door spiders don't build webs, but rather use their silk thread to build small tunnel-like burrows on the ground. At the end of the tunnel, they create a small "trap door" from silk. When an insect wanders by, the spider opens the door, snags the insect, and pulls it into the tunnel to be eaten.

Scientists have found a way to produce large quantities of spider silk. They have altered the DNA of some goats so that they produce silk in their milk. Because of its strength, this goat silk should have many uses in industries where a light but strong material is needed.

How does a spider create a web?

On an early morning walk, you may have spotted a spider's web covered with dew. The tiny droplets of water can make the details of a web very visible. If you had taken a moment to examine it, you might have seen what an amazing feat of engineering a spider's web is.

Spiders produce silk from **spinneret** glands located in the abdomen. They can produce a variety of different types of silk, depending on how it will be used. For example, sticky silk captures prey, but other types of silk are used for protecting eggs or constructing a web. The silk is very light but also incredibly strong. You may have heard that a piece of steel the same thickness as a spider's thread isn't as strong. That is true. Human beings have created nothing that is as lightweight and strong as spider's silk.

The most common type of web is the circular orb web. The first step in building this type of web is for a spider to release a single thread and wait for the wind to catch it. When a breeze attaches the fine piece of silk to a nearby surface, the spider travels across this bridge, reinforcing it with another thread. It then spins more silk to create a y-shaped line suspended from the bridge.

The spider continues weaving, adding more spokes, or **radials**, to the web. Once this section of the web is complete, the spider can begin creating the spiral portion of the web that connects the radials. Within the web, the spider includes non-sticky threads that it can use during the web's construction. It will often consume these threads before construction is finished.

After about an hour's work, the spider has completed the web. The size of the web and how tightly it is woven depend upon the size of the spider and of the prey it plans to catch. Some spiders wait quietly near the center of the web for an unsuspecting insect to become trapped, while others hide out of sight. Some spin a signal thread which will vibrate when an insect has been trapped and alert the spider to its presence.

Even though creating a web uses a lot of energy, new orb webs are constructed almost every day. If an insect damages a web, the spider may try to repair it. Otherwise, the spider will often eat the silk threads and begin work on a new web the following day.

Write **true** or **false** next to each statement below.

1. _____ All spiders spin webs.

2. _____ Most orb webs are rebuilt every day.

3. _____ Spiders can produce different types of silk from their spinnerets.

4. _____ Spider silk is weak, but similar silk produced by goats is much stronger.

5. _____ A spider that catches small insects, like gnats, will have a tightly woven web.

Write your answers on the lines below.

6. Do you think that a spider web is a more efficient means of capturing prey than chasing it? Explain.

_____

_____

7. Explain how spiders can use vibrations to help them capture their prey.

_____

8. How can goats create silk protein?

_____

9. Why do you think the author of the selection calls spider webs an "amazing feat of engineering"?

_____

_____

Unifying Concepts and Processes

Scientists believe that the evolution of flying insects and spiders may have influenced one another. If the earliest spiders built their webs near the ground, insects that could fly would be less likely to become trapped. How do you think this affected the behavior of spiders?

_____

_____

Journey for Survival

migration: the seasonal journey of an animal between two locations

instinctual: driven by an inborn, unlearned behavior

temperate: pleasant; mild or moderate

dwindling: decreasing or running out

Each year in the fall, adult female eels journey from freshwater lakes and rivers to the Sargasso Sea so they can breed with the male eels that live in the coastal waters. They lay their eggs in the ocean because the eel larvae cannot survive in freshwater. When they are grown, the eels move back to the freshwater lakes and rivers.

Some birds follow a unique pattern of migration. They journey east to west to spend the winter on the coast. Other birds live at high altitudes in the mountains and avoid harsh winters by moving lower into the valleys.

Why do some animals make journeys that are thousands of miles long every year?

Have you ever watched a flock of geese heading south in the fall and wondered how they know it's time to go? The geese are following their natural instinct to migrate. **Migration** is the **instinctual** journey of an animal traveling between two locations, often seasonally.

What is the advantage of such a long journey? Some of the reasons animals migrate are to find food or a more **temperate** climate, or to give birth. Many birds travel from their northern summer homes to their southern winter homes in order to avoid harsh climates. The Arctic tern, a relative of the seagull, is an amazing migrator. Each year, terns fly more than 12,000 miles round trip between the Arctic and the Antarctic. Flying as much as 200 miles per day, the terns migrate farther than any other animal. When they arrive in Antarctica, it is December, when the summer days are long due to the tilt of the planet. As long nights return to Antarctica, the terns fly north to the Arctic summer.

Birds are not the only animals to migrate. Many species of fish migrate, returning to the exact location where they were born. Salmon swim upstream from saltwater to fresh water, struggling against the current in order to deposit and fertilize their eggs. Many salmon die after their exhausting trip.

The Serengeti wildebeests of Africa must migrate in order to survive the inhospitable climate, lack of water, **dwindling** food supply, and predators. These animals travel a circle of 500 to 1,000 miles per year as they constantly seek a fresh source of food and a safe place to give birth.

Many migrating animals actually travel the same path each cycle. But how do they know the way? Scientists believe birds are able to use the position of the sun and stars to locate their path. They also memorize the terrain of the land below them, as well as the smells and even sounds along the route. Fish, whales, and dolphins take note of the direction, speed, depth, and smell of underwater currents.

Scientists are still trying to understand all the mysteries of migration. By catching migratory animals and tagging them with electronic transmitters, scientists can track migration patterns after the animals are released. This allows them to learn more about the behaviors that drive these animals on their long journeys.

Circle the letter of the best answer to each question below.

1. Why do salmon migrate?

   a. to escape predators

   b. to lay their eggs

   c. to search for better sources of food

   d. because the waters where they were born become too cold in winter

2. Which of the following is not used by animals to travel the same migratory path each year?

   a. memory

   b. the position of celestial bodies

   c. the shape of the land

   d. cloud patterns

Write your answers on the lines below.

3. Explain how you think migration might affect animals in a food chain.

   _____

   _____

4. How has technology allowed scientists to study migration?

   _____

5. Why do you think some animals migrate while others are able to live in the same place year round?

   _____

6. Animals aren't the only creatures that migrate. Some groups of human beings who live off the land also migrate. Based on the selection, give two reasons they might do so.

   _____

What's Next?

Not all migrations are round-trip migrations. Do some research about nomadic migrations, irruption, and removal or one-way migrations. How do the reasons for these migrations differ from those of round-trip migrators?

abstract: relating to a concept, like love or honesty, rather than something concrete, like an apple or a ball

ethologists: scientists who study animal behavior

A large brain relative to the size of an animal's body is one indication of intelligence. This ratio is the largest for human beings, followed by bottlenose dolphins and chimpanzees. Although brain size is one indicator of intelligence, scientists have found behavior to be a more useful measure.

A dolphin named *Kelly* impressed researchers in Mississippi by devising a way to get more fish. When she caught a gull passing overhead, she was rewarded with fish. She saved a fish and used it as bait to catch another gull, which meant that she was rewarded with more fish. She later taught this clever strategy to her offspring, who taught it to other dolphins at the center.

How do human beings measure intelligence in animals?

Scientists have a series of qualities they use to determine a species's intelligence—a difficult concept to measure, especially in animals. Problem-solving abilities and use of tools are two qualities scientists evaluate. Understanding language and **abstract** concepts, as well as having a sense of self-awareness, are also linked to intelligence. Because these are difficult things to measure, scientists must carefully observe behaviors and be creative with the experiments they design.

Primates have long been thought to be the most intelligent mammals besides human beings. Much of what is known about chimpanzees comes from Jane Goodall's extensive observation of them in the wild. One startling discovery she made was that chimps use tools like twigs and long grasses to fish termites from their nests. In recent years, they have also been seen making spears for hunting. Before Goodall's discoveries, scientists believed that only human beings created weapons and tools.

As the study of animal intelligence has grown, other species have also been observed making tools. In Australia, some dolphins use natural sponges to cover their snouts and protect themselves from spiny fish. Some crows use sticks to retrieve insects to eat, similar to chimpanzees.

Language and communication are also studied by **ethologists** searching for clues to animal intelligence. Both dolphins and primates have been trained in sign language and can recognize individual words, as well as the combination of a series of words in sentences. A study done with dolphins revealed that they even have some concept of mathematics. After training, they were able to identify the concept of "fewer" using display boards that showed different numbers of dots.

One of the classic tests of intelligence is to make a mark on an animal while it is asleep. When an intelligent animal is shown its reflection in a mirror, it will notice the mark and begin grooming that area of its body. This occurs in chimps, apes, and dolphins. A less intelligent animal may notice the mark but be unaware that it is seeing its reflection.

Scientists won't likely discover levels of animal intelligence approaching human levels. Instead, researchers hope to learn more about the ways in which animals are intelligent and how human beings may be able to communicate with them. This can also help scientists gain a better understanding of human intelligence and how it evolved.

Write **true** or **false** next to each statement below.

1. _____ Brain size is the only indicator scientists have of an animal's intelligence.

2. _____ Pleasure is an example of an abstract concept.

3. _____ Neither primates nor dolphins are able to recognize themselves when shown their reflections in a mirror.

4. _____ Learning about animal intelligence may be able to help scientists better understand how human intelligence evolved.

5. _____ Only human beings and dolphins make and use tools.

Write your answers on the lines below.

6. Name three qualities scientists look for when measuring animal intelligence.

_____

7. Explain how the "mirror test" identifies self-awareness in animals.

_____

_____

8. Why do you think that showing an understanding of abstract concepts is an indication of intelligence?

_____

_____

9. Explain how Kelly the dolphin exhibited problem-solving behaviors.

_____

_____

10. Why was the use of tools and weapons by chimps an important discovery for scientists?

_____

Standing Tall and Strong

Why are some of the world's most beautiful forests at risk?

Visit some of the cooler regions of the Northern Hemisphere, and you'll see some of the world's most beautiful forests. Coniferous forests cover about 15 percent of the land on Earth. They are populated by **conifers**—trees that usually have needles instead of leaves, and cones instead of flowers. Pines, firs, cypresses, junipers, and redwoods are all examples of conifers that might be familiar to you. Instead of shedding their leaves in autumn as **deciduous** trees do, most conifers are evergreen and keep their needles for three or four years. Some species shed their needles only once every 15 years.

The locations of most coniferous forests require the trees to be hardy. They must be able to withstand cold temperatures, heavy snows, rocky soil, and summer forest fires. Several adaptations allow them to do this. For example, thick bark on the trees' trunks keeps them from sustaining too much damage during nearby forest fires. They also contain resins, chemicals that emit a strong scent. Insects are repelled by the odor, which helps protect conifers from insect damage.

California redwoods, also called *sequoias*, are some of the hardiest conifers. Their strength is evident in their life span, which may be more than 3,000 years long. The giant trees can grow to more than 300 feet in height with a trunk diameter of about 35 feet. Like other conifers, resistance to insects and fires contribute to their ability to survive.

Coniferous forests, like many other green spaces, are in danger of destruction. **Clear-cutting** forests to make room for human development, like new roads and housing, can mean the loss of thousands of trees. It can also mean the loss of habitat for many animals, such as bald eagles, bears, moose, squirrels, big-horned sheep, and owls.

One alternative to clear-cutting forests is called *selective logging*. Instead of cutting down all the trees in an area, a number of diverse trees are spared. This ensures that the members of the local animal population don't lose their homes and that some of each native species of tree is preserved.

Coniferous forests are also at risk for damage caused by acid rain and the increasing temperatures associated with global warming. While these are serious environmental problems, the actions of individuals can make a difference. Even small changes—like walking instead of driving or lowering the thermostat—can create big changes when many people take part.

NAME _____

Circle the letter of the best answer to the question below.

1. Which of the following is a characteristic of a coniferous forest biome?

    a. southern locations and warm, moist weather

    b. poor, rocky soil

    c. northern locations and cool temperatures

    d. Both b and c

Write your answers on the lines below.

2. How are coniferous and deciduous trees different from one another?

    _____

    _____

3. Choose two adaptations that conifers have, and explain how they help the trees survive.

    _____

    _____

4. What is clear-cutting? Explain why selective logging is a healthier choice for the environment.

    _____

    _____

    _____

5. What are two risks to the health of coniferous forests besides clear-cutting?

    _____

6. Explain how forest fires are part of the life cycle of the lodgepole pine.

    _____

    _____

7. What can people do to help preserve coniferous forests?

    _____

Circle the letter of the best answer to each question below.

1. _____ are logical subjects to use in a study of genetics and nature versus nurture.

   a. Identical twins

   b. People with very high IQs

   c. Adopted children

   d. Both a and c

2. Why have scientists been experimenting with finding a way for animals, such as goats, to produce spider silk?

   a. because the silk improves the quality of goats' milk

   b. because spider silk contains chemicals that can benefit the health of other animals

   c. because spiders have been producing less silk in recent years

   d. because spider silk is incredibly strong and has many potential uses

3. A researcher makes a white mark on the face of a chimp while it is asleep. When the chimp awakens, it is shown a mirror and immediately rubs at the mark. This shows

   a. an ability to communicate with human beings.

   b. self-awareness and intelligencc.

   c. that the chimp thinks it is pointing out the mark to another chimp.

   d. None of the above

Underline the correct answer from the two choices you are given.

4. Most of a cell's activities are controlled by the (nucleus, ribosomes).

5. (Diffusion, Equilibrium) describes a stable, balanced system.

6. (Cartilaginous, Synovial) joints allow the back to bend.

7. Some people who take (probiotics, antibiotics) also take (probiotics, antibiotics) to replenish their supply of "good" bacteria.

8. Plants that have needles and cones are known as (deciduous, coniferous) trees.

9. Human beings have the ability to understand (abstract, concrete) concepts, like truth.

Write your answers on the lines below.

10. How is a cell like a living organism?

_____

11. Why do plant cells contain chloroplasts and animal cells do not?

_____

12. Give two examples of how homeostasis helps regulate the human body.

_____

13. Explain the concept of nature versus nurture.

_____

14. How is a ball-and-socket joint, like a hip joint, different from a hinge joint, like an elbow joint?

_____

15. What effect does arthritis have on the body?

_____

16. How did observation play an important role in the discovery of penicillin?

_____

_____

17. What are two uses, besides web construction, that spiders have for their silk?

_____

18. Give three examples of reasons that a species of animal might migrate.

_____

19. Explain what it means to say that migration is an "instinctual journey."

_____

20. What are two behaviors observed in chimpanzees that indicate high intelligence?

_____

Underline the correct answer from the two choices you are given.

1. (Parallax, Spectroscopy) is used to determine how far away stars are.

2. Enzymes are (catalysts, organelles) that help cells make energy.

3. Most metals oxidize easily because they are (malleable, reactive).

4. Copper exposed to air will turn green because of (oxidation, conductivity).

5. The law of (inertia, entropy) states that matter always moves toward a state of balance.

6. Mitochondria, lysosomes, and vacuoles are (organelles, proteins) inside cells.

7. (Ethologists, Anthropologists) are scientists who study animal behavior.

Write **true** or **false** next to each statement below.

8. _____ There have been about 15 mass extinctions throughout history.

9. _____ Equal concentrations of either salt or sugar in water will lower the freezing point of water the same amount.

10. _____ The rings of a tree can offer information about weather conditions in various years.

11. _____ Blue mussels evolved a defense mechanism to crabs in the span of just 15 years.

12. _____ About three-quarters of the elements are metals.

13. _____ Matter can undergo a physical or chemical change, but not both at the same time.

14. _____ Scientists understand the effects of gravity, but they don't know what causes it.

15. _____ Perfect vacuums don't exist naturally.

16. _____ In the spectrum, longer wavelengths contain more energy than shorter ones.

17. _____ Every proton is made up of three smaller particles, called *quarks*.

18. _____ Joints are classified by the amount of movement they allow.

19. _____ Good bacteria live inside your body and help with digestion.

Write your answers on the lines below.

20. Why was there debate about whether *Homo floresiensis* should be considered a separate species from *Homo sapiens*?

_____

21. List two reasons a scientist should know how to use a computer.

_____

22. What discovery did the Leakeys make that supported their belief that Africa, not Asia, was "the cradle of humanity"?

_____

23. How did Joseph Lister decrease the mortality rate in his hospital?

_____

24. _____ and _____ are the longest living organisms on Earth.

25. List three signs that indicate a chemical change has taken place.

_____   _____   _____

26. Explain why a ship made of iron will float, but a small, solid chunk of iron will sink.

_____

_____

27. Objects A and B have equal volumes and are both traveling at 25 miles per hour. Object A is much denser than Object B. Which object has a greater amount of force and why?

_____

28. Breathing harder when you exercise is an example of _____.

29. The debate about whether heredity or environment is more important is referred to as

_____ versus _____.

30. Why do animals migrate? Give at least three reasons.

_____

_____

Lesson 4.1   Frozen in Time

ice age: a period of cooling in Earth's history when much of the surface of the planet is covered by glaciers

plate tectonics: the theory that Earth's crust is divided into segments called *plates*, which are constantly shifting and moving over the surface of the planet

During the most recent North American ice age, the Wisconsin glaciation, the climate was wetter and average temperatures were about 30°F colder.

Fossils are an important element in the study of ice ages. Fossils of plants and animals that live in cold climates today have been found in more temperate regions. This indicates that at some point in history, those regions were colder than they are today. Dating fossils can help scientists pinpoint that time in history.

What causes ice ages to occur, and how often do they take place?

If you ever read the newspaper or watch the national news, you've probably heard of global warming—the scientific theory that the temperatures on Earth are slowly rising, at least partly due to human activity. It might come as a surprise to you, then, that our planet is currently in the middle of an **ice age**. How could both things be happening at once?

An ice age is a time period in Earth's history when there is a decrease in the average temperatures and when large parts of Earth's surface are covered by sheets of ice, called *glaciers*. During the last billion years, our planet has experienced about five major ice ages. Each one lasts millions of years.

Within that time, there are shorter cycles when the ice sheets advance and then retreat. These cycles may last for 100,000 years, with warming periods lasting about 10,000 years. Scientists believe that the most recent major ice age began 2.5 million years ago and last peaked about 20,000 years ago. Currently, Earth is in a warmer phase of the ice age. It has lasted for longer than 10,000 years, though, so a cooler phase may be on the horizon.

Instead of seeing temperatures begin to slowly decrease as you might expect, they are actually on the rise. Most of the scientific community is in agreement that global warming exists and that it is caused in part by human beings' increased use of fossil fuels, which create greenhouse gases. Human activity may actually be changing a cycle that has been repeating itself for billions of years in Earth's history.

Scientist Louis Agassiz was the first to propose the idea of ice ages. As he studied glaciers in Switzerland in the 1800s, he found that they made noticeable changes in Earth's surface—like glacial lakes, erosion, and deposits. He found these same signs in places where there were no glaciers, which made him believe that glaciers might have existed there long ago. Modern scientists have found many other indicators since that time to confirm Agassiz's ideas.

Even today, scientists don't know exactly why ice ages occur. What they do know is that a variety of factors are involved. They believe that **plate tectonics** is likely to play a role. Changes in Earth's orbit, in the level of the seas, and in the amount of energy the sun produces are also possibilities. As research continues, more pieces of the puzzle of Earth's natural history are sure to be found.

Circle the letter of the best answer to each question below.

1. Which of the following statements is not true?

   a. Most of Earth's surface is covered by glaciers for the entire length of an ice age.

   b. Scientists are not sure exactly what causes ice ages to occur.

   c. Earth is currently experiencing an ice age.

   d. Both a and b

2. Ice Ages last

   a. about 10,000 years.

   b. between 10,000 and 100,000 years.

   c. millions of years.

   d. billions of years.

PLEASE DO NOT WRITE ON THE PAGES IN THIS BOOK. MAKE PHOTOCOPIES OF THE ONES YOU NEED.

3. Which of the following is not one of the factors that scientists believe may cause ice ages to occur?

   a. plate tectonics

   b. changes in Earth's orbit

   c. changes in the amount of heat the sun produces

   d. global warming

Write your answers on the lines below.

4. Explain how Earth can be in the middle of an ice age at the same time it is experiencing global warming.

   _____

   _____

5. What led Louis Agassiz to form his theory about the existence of ice ages?

   _____

   _____

What's Next?

Find out more about the signs scientists use to learn about ice ages in Earth's history. What can they learn from ice cores, ocean sediments, and glaciers?

El Niño: Stirring Up Trouble Around the World

topographical maps: maps that show the terrain or ocean depths in three dimensions

La Niña is a weather-related event that often goes hand-in-hand with an El Niño. The winds are stronger during a La Niña, and the waters of the tropical Pacific are colder. This results in heavy rains in areas like Indonesia that experience drought during an El Niño.

El Niño, which means "boy child" in Spanish, was named by fishermen off the coast of Peru. They noticed that in late December every few years there was a warming of ocean waters that caused a sharp decrease in the number of fish they caught.

What causes an El Niño to take place, and what effects does it have?

Have you ever heard of El Niño? It's blamed for all sorts of weather events around the world, like hurricanes, droughts, and floods. El Niño begins in the Pacific Ocean. It's part of a weather phenomenon called *ENSO. EN* stands for "El Niño," and *SO* stands for "Southern Oscillation"—the pattern of reversing air pressure over the Pacific Ocean that causes an El Niño.

Near the equator, the surface temperature of the Pacific is usually quite warm. Strong winds push these warm surface waters from the coast of South America westward toward Australia. When this happens, cooler waters rise from deep in the ocean and take the place of the warmer surface waters.

During an El Niño, however, the winds are much weaker and can even blow in the opposite direction. Warm surface water pools at the equator near the coast of South America and then spreads north and south along the coastline of the Americas. The warm waters have the effect of weakening the wind, which causes the waters to become warmer. This back-and-forth relationship between air pressure and water temperature causes an El Niño to grow.

Another effect of the warm ocean waters is the formation of clouds that result in heavy rains and flooding in North and South America. During a severe El Niño of 1997 and 1998, about 15 times the normal amount of rain fell in Ecuador and Peru. It resulted in flooding, landslides, disease, and death. In other places in the world, El Niños result in droughts. In Indonesia, drought caused forest fires that did millions of dollars worth of damage and also caused loss of life. Crop production and fishermen around the world were also affected by the unusual weather and water conditions.

El Niños do not take place on a predictable schedule, but scientists have determined that they tend to occur every three to seven years and last about a year to a year and a half. To make things even more complicated, the conditions that accompany an El Niño vary and aren't always consistent.

One way in which scientists can study El Niños is by using satellite technology. They know that sea levels are slightly higher when ocean waters are warm and lower when the waters are cold. The satellites can take very precise measurements of the ocean levels, which allows scientists to create **topographical maps** charting the movement of El Niños.

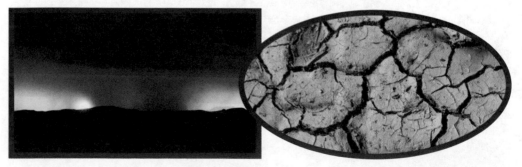

Circle the letter of the best answer to each question below.

1. Which of the following statements is true?

    a. La Niñas occur much less frequently than El Niños do.

    b. In normal conditions, winds push the warm waters of the tropical Pacific westward.

    c. El Niños occur precisely every three years.

    d. Both a and b

2. Why is El Niño considered to be a troublemaker?

    a. because scientists have to use satellites to chart its progress

    b. because it occurs every year late in December

    c. because it can cause droughts, flooding, and other extreme or unusual weather events

    d. because it prevents a La Niña from occurring

3. Which of the following most accurately describes El Niño?

    a. a weather phenomenon caused by flooding in the Americas and droughts in western tropical Pacific areas

    b. a weather phenomenon that results from changes in air pressure and water temperature over and in the Pacific Ocean

    c. a severe hurricane with intense winds and significant waves

    d. warm waters in the Atlantic Ocean that flow westward in heavy wind

Write your answers on the lines below.

4. Explain how a La Niña and an El Niño are similar and different.

    _____

    _____

5. How can the observations of nonscientists, like fisherman, be of value to scientists?

    _____

    _____

6. How can technology help scientists in their study of El Niño?

    _____

Mountain Mayhem

inclines: surfaces that lie at a slope, a slant, or an angle

accumulates: gathers or collects over a period of time

snowpack: an accumulation of packed snow that builds up in layers over time

compressed: pushed or pressed tightly together

climatologists: scientists who study climates and weather patterns

forecast: to predict using data and observations

If you are caught in an avalanche, experts suggest trying to "swim" on top of the snow using breaststroke motions.

Explosives are one method of preventing large avalanches from occurring. They are often used at ski resorts and in other populated mountain areas. Setting off controlled explosives triggers small avalanches and prevents the snow from accumulating enough for larger, more destructive avalanches to take place. Snow fences, large nets, and the preserving or planting of trees can also help prevent or lessen the effects of avalanches.

What happens when an avalanche strikes?

In 1970, an avalanche in the mountains of Peru tumbled 13,200 feet and killed more than 18,000 people in the valley below. During World War I, avalanches triggered by nearby artillery fire claimed the lives of more than 50,000 soldiers in Austria and Italy. Avalanches can be a spectacular force of nature—as well as an extremely dangerous one.

An avalanche happens when snow, or even rock and soil, slide down the side of a mountain. While you might think that avalanches would be caused by snow tumbling down very steep mountainsides, it actually doesn't accumulate as deeply on steeper slopes. Ninety percent of avalanches happen on average **inclines** of 30 to 45 degrees.

As snow **accumulates** on the ground, many layers create a **snowpack**. Changes in temperature can cause ice crystals to form, which prevents the snow from sticking together. This results in a weak layer of snow that will slide easily. The location of the weak layer determines the type of avalanche.

There are two kinds of avalanches—sluffs and slabs. A snowpack topped by a weak layer of snow is called a *sluff*. A sluff avalanche does not contain a large amount of snow because the snow is powdery and loose. Damage is minimal from a sluff avalanche. The more common slab avalanches can occur when a weak layer forms in the middle of the snowpack. On top of the weak layer, there are many **compressed** layers of snow. When it is triggered, this layer slides down the slope, bringing with it all of the snow on top. Slab avalanches can move as fast as 200 miles an hour.

Of course, the snowpack would remain stable if nothing caused it to move. Avalanches are triggered by vibrations from loud noises, changes in temperature, and earthquake activity that disturbs the weak layer.

Unfortunately, it is not yet possible for geologists, engineers, and **climatologists** to predict exact avalanche locations. Experts are, however, able to **forecast** hazard levels based on periodic checks of the snowpack, temperature, and wind conditions. Researchers dig snow pits several feet square near an area that is likely to have an avalanche. They examine the layers of the snowpack, and tell how stable they are. If the area looks unsafe, warnings can be issued until conditions improve.

Circle the letter of the best answer to each question below.

1. Which of the following is not likely to trigger an avalanche?

   a. an earthquake

   b. an explosion

   c. a sudden increase in temperatures

   d. a person skiing on freshly-fallen snow

2. Which statement is true?

   a. Layers of packed snow are referred to as *snowpack* and can help scientists forecast avalanches.

   b. Trees increase the likelihood of an avalanche taking place.

   c. A weak layer of snow is always found at the bottom of snowpack.

   d. Both a and b

Write your answers on the lines below.

3. Explain why damage is more likely to result from a slab avalanche than a sluff avalanche.

   _____

   _____

4. Why are avalanches more likely to occur on mountains that do not have very steep inclines?

   _____

5. Why do you think avalanches can't be precisely predicted?

   _____

6. How do scientists identify avalanche hazard levels?

   _____

7. Why are explosives used to create avalanches?

   _____

   _____

Flowing Underground

groundwater: water that lies below Earth's surface; in some areas, it may be frozen

saturation: the point at which something is completely full

aquifer: a saturated layer of soil, sand, or gravel that provides a supply of usable water

impermeable: not allowing passage through

Groundwater that lies deep underground may not make its way to the surface for thousands or even millions of years.

An aquitard is a layer of material that slows the flow of groundwater. It's made of dense materials like clay or shale. An aquiclude is an **impermeable** layer of material through which groundwater cannot pass.

Groundwater stays relatively close to Earth's surface and lies no more than a few miles below ground. Rock found deeper than that is too dense to allow groundwater to seep into it or flow through it.

What role does groundwater play in the water cycle?

What lies below the surface of Earth? If you were to start digging, you'd find a mixture of soil, gravel, sand, and rocks, depending on the region of the country. If you kept on digging, sooner or later you'd find water. In some places, like wetlands, water lies just below the surface. In other parts of the world, such as deserts, it may be several hundred feet below ground. As you may have already guessed, **groundwater** is simply water that lies below Earth's surface.

The source of most groundwater is precipitation in the form of rain, snow, hail, and sleet. As the precipitation seeps into the ground, it is drawn deeper by the pull of gravity. It fills the spaces between the grains of sand, gravel, or soil. It even seeps into the tiny pores and crevices in rocks. When an area is completely filled with water, it has reached the zone of **saturation**. The top of this saturated zone is called the *water table*. During times of drought or when people are overusing the water supply, the water table drops significantly.

Earth has about 100 times more groundwater than fresh surface water in lakes and rivers. It can be used in households for bathing or drinking, in industry, and to irrigate crops. A well is used to bring groundwater to the surface. The well reaches water in an **aquifer**—a saturated layer of material, like gravel or sand, that holds water.

Groundwater tends to be cleaner than surface water because it is protected from waste and contaminants in the air. This doesn't mean, unfortunately, that groundwater isn't subject to pollution. Tanks that store gas underground can leak and pollute groundwater. Chemicals can seep from landfills and add to underground pollution, as can runoff from fertilizers used in farming. It is not uncommon for wells to be closed because the groundwater they pump is too contaminated to be useful.

Like other water on Earth, groundwater is a part of the hydrologic, or water, cycle. It just moves more slowly through the cycle than surface water. After it seeps deep into the ground, it flows slowly through layers of rock and soil. Eventually, it is discharged into springs, streams, lakes, and even the oceans. From these bodies of water, it evaporates, condenses and forms clouds, and then falls again to the ground as precipitation. As it soaks into the ground, the cycle begins again.

Water Table

Saturated Zone (Aquifer)

NAME _____

Underline the correct answer from the two choices you are given.

1. A well taps groundwater in an (aquiclude, aquifer).

2. Water cannot pass through (an impermeable, a permeable) layer of material.

3. Human beings can access groundwater by using (wells, landfills) to pump the water to the surface.

4. The material in an aquifer is (irrigated, saturated) with water.

Write your answers on the lines below.

5. If groundwater is located below Earth's surface, how can it be a part of the water cycle?

_____

_____

6. What are three ways in which groundwater is used?

_____

7. Why isn't groundwater found in all of Earth's layers?

_____

8. What could cause the water table to drop?

_____

9. How do you think the groundwater supply differs from a dry, hot area, like Arizona, to a cooler, moist area, like Oregon? Where do you think the water table is lower?

_____

_____

What's Next?

Do some research about natural springs. What causes groundwater to be discharged from the earth at the source of a spring? How is the water in a hot spring heated?

Everything Falls Apart

decomposed: broken down into individual chemical components; rotted or decayed

mechanical weathering: weathering that causes a physical change

chemical weathering: weathering that causes a chemical change

lichens: complex organisms that are made up of fungi and algae that exist together in a relationship that benefits both

Interesting landforms are created when a variety of rock types are layered together. The various layers weather in different ways and at different rates. The result is often a rock face striped by various shades and colors. Ledges or shelves appear when a layer weathers more quickly than the one above it.

An outcropping is an exposed area of bedrock. Bedrock is the layer, or layers, of rock usually found underground, and therefore exposed to much less weathering. Bedrock often contains geological information that's millions, or even billions, of years old.

How does solid rock turn into soil?

Entropy is the second law of thermodynamics, which states that everything in the universe naturally moves toward a state of equilibrium. Molecules that are organized into larger matter—whether it's a book, a planet's atmosphere, or a glass of water—will eventually break apart, become disorganized, and spread evenly through space. That's entropy, and on Earth, weathering plays a big role in ensuring that the second law of thermodynamics is carried out.

You might think that the biggest, most solid rocks on or near Earth's surface would be permanent fixtures. Over time, though, weathering breaks them down into increasingly smaller pieces. Eventually, they end up as tiny grains of sand, which mix with **decomposed** plant and animal material to form soil. This process is a vital part of life on Earth because, without soil, most plants can't grow on land.

Mechanical weathering causes physical changes in rocks. For example, changing temperatures can cause a rock to expand or contract, creating small cracks in the rock's surface. When water seeps into these cracks and freezes, it expands and makes the cracks wider. This cycle continues until the rock breaks apart. Salt crystals forming inside these cracks can also create destructive pressures. The freeze-thaw cycle and salts used to melt snow are the main reasons cracks and potholes appear regularly in our roadways.

Chemical weathering occurs when a rock's surface reacts with chemicals in the atmosphere. A rock's exposed surface will oxidize when it comes into contact with oxygen, water, carbon dioxide, or acid rain. For example, a red rock most likely contains iron oxide, or rust. Chemical changes can make a rock soft enough to be broken by hand, or it can smooth sharp edges and alter a rock's shape without breaking it into pieces. Chemical weathering also affects old stone buildings and statues by eating holes in them.

Plants and animals cause biological weathering. Plants' roots grow down into cracks in a rock and force them open. **Lichens** growing on a rock's surface consume minerals and break it apart, molecule by molecule.

Although erosion and weathering are related, they aren't the same thing. After weathering has broken a rock into small pieces, wind or water will carry them away. Erosion moves weathered materials from place to place—one more way the world tends toward entropy.

Circle the letter of the best answer to each question below.

1. Water seeps into a crack in a rock, freezes, expands, and causes the crack to widen. This is an example of

   a. mechanical weathering.

   b. chemical weathering.

   c. erosion.

   d. All of the above

2. When weathering causes a copper statue to change from a shiny, golden-brown color to a dull, greenish-brown color, the statue has

   a. experienced chemical weathering.

   b. undergone a physical change.

   c. been affected by oxidation.

   d. All of the above

Write your answers on the lines below.

3. Would a cliff in the desert or a cliff along the seashore experience more weathering? Explain your answer.

   _____

   _____

4. How are erosion and weathering different?

   _____

   _____

5. Why are outcroppings important places for geological study?

   _____

Unifying Concepts and Processes

A rock's volume changes depending on the temperature. Does a rock expand or contract with an increase in heat? Explain how you know.

_____

_____

Crystal Clear

crystals: solid matter formed by a repeating, three-dimensional pattern of bonded molecules

crystallize: to form crystals

symmetrical: having symmetry, which is matching shapes or parts arranged equally on opposite sides of a boundary

crystalline: like a crystal

minerals: solid, inorganic elements or compounds that have crystalline structures and contain only a single element or compound

cleave: to split or break apart along a natural dividing line

Rocks and minerals aren't the same thing. Minerals, like quartz or salt, contain just one substance arranged in a crystal structure. Rocks are aggregates, or clusters, of many different minerals. Some rocks, like coal, also contain the remains of once-living organisms.

One characteristic of crystals is that they **cleave**, or split, easily. Striking a crystal in just the right place will cause it to break along one of its internal borders. Each piece of the broken crystal will have smooth faces, just as the original whole did.

What makes a crystal different from any other rock?

The sparkling gemstones displayed in a jewelry shop window come in various shapes, sizes, and colors. Beautiful **crystals**, such as diamonds, rubies, and sapphires, might lead you to believe that all crystals are rare and expensive, but they're actually pretty common. In fact, most substances **crystallize** when the right conditions are present.

The atoms and molecules in all solids are densely packed together, but the molecules in crystals are bonded together in a way that creates **symmetrical** shapes, like cubes. These tiny, individual shapes combine in a repeating pattern to create the larger **crystalline** structure. Imagine the individual hexagons that make up a honeycomb. A crystal's structure is similar, but in three dimensions.

Crystals often form when high concentrations of molecules in a solution have very little energy. If there's a lot of heat, the energized molecules will be too active to come together. When molecules are packed tightly together and have low energy, groups of them will naturally begin to form bonds. They come together in tiny, symmetrical units that combine to create a crystal. The crystal continues growing until all the molecules have become part of the structure, or until the concentration of molecules in the solution is no longer dense enough to cause further crystallization.

Earth's **minerals** are crystals that formed deep underground during a period of millions of years. It's not particularly cool down there, but the pressure is intense enough to force molecules together and cause crystallization. Diamonds, for example, are carbon atoms that crystallized due to the pressures found about 100 miles below Earth's surface.

Some crystals form much more quickly. Snowflakes and ice are examples of water crystallizing in a very short time. When temperatures drop to freezing, water molecules have very little energy and begin bonding to each other. The beautiful structure of a snowflake is tiny symmetrical water crystals combining to form a larger symmetrical shape.

Although rocks and metals aren't crystals, crystals are still a part of their structures. If you look at a rock or a piece of metal under a microscope, you'll see that they both contain many tiny individual crystals that are clumped together randomly.

Circle the letter of the best answer to each question below.

1. Which of the following statements is true?

    a. All crystals are used for jewelry.

    b. Crystals form only in freezing temperatures.

    c. All crystals were formed deep within Earth.

    d. Diamonds are crystals formed from carbon atoms.

2. Sodium chloride, or table salt, has a crystalline structure. This means

    a. it cannot be dissolved in water.

    b. its molecules bonded to form symmetrical solids.

    c. it cannot undergo any further chemical changes.

    d. All of the above

3. Metals contain crystals, but they're not crystals themselves, because

    a. the individual symmetrical solids do not form a repeated pattern.

    b. the crystals have changed chemically and become rocks.

    c. the crystals in metals are not made of molecules.

    d. they do not reflect light.

Write your answers on the lines below.

4. Is a diamond a mineral? Why or why not?

    _____

    _____

5. Explain the difference between a rock and a mineral.

    _____

What's Next?

The Mohs scale of mineral hardness ranks minerals according to their ability to scratch each other. The hardest substance on Earth is the diamond—it scratches all other substances. Find a copy of Mohs scale and see how other minerals rank.

It Begins with a Bang

celestial: relating to the sky or space

Big Bang Theory: the widely accepted theory that the universe began as a single piece of matter that exploded and expanded—and is still expanding today; nearly all astronomical evidence supports this theory

gravitationally-bound: held together by gravitational forces

galaxies: gravitationally-bound groups of millions or billions of stars

entity: a distinct, individual thing

condense: make more dense or compact

The universe appears to have vast amounts of emptiness in between its clusters, galaxies, and solar systems, but scientists know better. All that empty space contains dark matter and dark energy. They're considered "dark" because they don't emit or reflect electromagnetic energy that we can see or detect. They do exert gravitational forces, though, which is how scientists know they must exist.

Where did the objects in our solar system come from?

Most scientists agree that all the particles in the universe were originally compressed into a single, extraordinarily hot and dense point of matter. Then, almost 14 billion years ago, this point exploded and the particles shot out in every direction to begin forming the universe.

In the first one-hundredth of a second after the explosion, the universe was an intensely hot soup of quarks, electrons, and electromagnetic energy. As the matter continued to expand, though, it quickly cooled, and the particles combined to form atoms. Over time, these atoms collected together into larger pieces of matter, which in turn combined to form the stars, planets, moons, and all the other **celestial** objects. This process is known as the **Big Bang Theory** of our universe's origins.

If matter had simply spread evenly throughout the universe, there would be only one atom in every cubic foot. Instead, forces—especially gravity—caused matter to combine into the objects and groups of objects that astronomers have been observing for centuries. Between these objects are what appear to be vast distances of nearly empty space.

The universe's largest, **gravitationally-bound** objects are clusters. A cluster contains hundreds, or even thousands, of **galaxies** moving as a single **entity** across space. Clusters form because of the gravitational forces the galaxies exert on each other. The smallest clusters are usually referred to more simply as *groups*.

The Milky Way galaxy contains at least 200 billion stars, and our sun is an average star located about three-quarters of the way toward the galaxy's outer edge. As the Milky Way rotates, it carries our sun and the entire solar system around its center once every 250 million years or so.

Our solar system is defined by the area of space and all the objects affected by the sun's gravity. About four and a half billion years ago, our sun formed, like most stars do, when gravity caused a gigantic cloud of dust and gas to **condense** into a burning sphere of matter. Whatever gas and dust didn't become part of the sun itself were captured by its gravity. Slowly, over the course of millions of years, gravity caused this orbiting matter to pull together to form clumps of various sizes—the planets and their moons. Billions of smaller objects remained unattached and are known today as asteroids, meteors, comets, and space dust.

Circle the letter of the best answer to each question below.

1. The Milky Way is

    a. a cluster.

    b. a Local Group.

    c. a galaxy.

    d. All of the above

2. Scientists theorize that the original point of matter from which our universe formed was smaller than a dime. This matter would also have

    a. had unimaginable mass.

    b. been incredibly dense.

    c. had unbelievable potential energy.

    d. All of the above

Write your answers on the lines below.

3. Could the universe have formed without gravity? Why or why not?

    _____

4. Which came into existence first—atoms or quarks? Explain your answer.

    _____

5. In your own words, describe the origins of the universe according to the Big Bang Theory.

    _____

    _____

6. Do you think the way a planet's moons form is similar to or different from the way the planets formed around the sun? Explain your answer.

    _____

    _____

    _____

satellite: a body that is in orbit around a larger body

axis: an imaginary straight line running from pole to pole around which a body rotates

analysis: a method of study that involves looking at specific features and seeing how they work together as a whole

molten: turned to liquid because of heat

magma: molten rock

The moon is about 239,000 miles from Earth, but each year it moves about an inch and a half farther away.

The moon has no atmosphere to protect it, so any object that crosses its path strikes the lunar surface and forms a crater. No atmosphere also means no wind or weather, so the moon's surface seldom changes.

From 1969 to 1972, the Apollo space program sent twelve different men to the moon. The last person to stand on the lunar surface was astronaut Eugene Cernan in December 1972.

Where did the moon come from?

Soon after telescopes were invented 400 years ago, Galileo Galilei focused his gaze on the biggest, brightest object in the night sky—the moon. He was able to make out a rough surface of mountains and craters covering Earth's only natural **satellite**. Until then, most people had assumed the moon was a smooth sphere. Galileo's closer look revealed that it wasn't as different from Earth as people had thought.

Month after month, the moon makes its way around our planet, completing one orbit every 27.3 days. Although from Earth it appears that the amount of sunlight hitting the moon is always changing, in reality, one half of the moon is always in sunlight, while the other half is in darkness. Lunar phases occur because we can see more or less of the lit half depending on where the moon is in its orbit.

Like Earth, the moon rotates on its **axis**, but a lunar day is much longer than an Earth day. Each lunar day is actually equal to the amount of time it takes the moon to orbit Earth—27.3 days. In other words, each time the moon orbits our planet, it also turns once on its axis. What this unique characteristic means is that the same side of the moon always ends up facing Earth as it orbits.

For centuries, myths were used to explain how the moon ended up in the sky. Scientists still don't know for certain what the moon's origins are, but several scientific hypotheses have been proposed, and one in particular is widely accepted.

In the past, it's been suggested that the moon was simply captured by Earth's gravity as it passed by. Others wondered if the moon formed from debris orbiting Earth, just as the planets formed around the sun. The biggest clue, though, came from **analysis** of the moon's composition. Scientists saw that both Earth and the moon are made of the same elements. This discovery led to the giant impact hypothesis.

Today, most scientists think that a Mars-sized object crashed into Earth about 4.5 billion years ago. This event caused a giant chunk of our planet to break away and move into orbit. The intense heat and energy from the collision meant that a **molten** sea of **magma** covered the moon in its earliest days. It slowly cooled over billions of years to become the quiet, familiar sphere that crosses our skies night after night.

Circle the letter of the best answer to each question below.

1. Lunar phases are a result of

   a. Earth's shadow being cast on the moon.

   b. the moon's changing position in relation to Earth and the sun.

   c. changes in the amount of sunlight hitting the moon.

   d. sunlight reflecting off Earth and hitting the moon.

2. The same side of the moon always faces Earth because

   a. the moon does not rotate as it orbits Earth.

   b. the moon's gravitational force isn't nearly as strong as Earth's.

   c. gravity from Mars pulls against the moon with a force equal to Earth's gravity.

   d. the moon completes just one rotation each time it orbits Earth.

Write your answers on the lines below.

3. Describe two ways in which Earth and its moon are similar.

   _____

   _____

4. Describe two ways in which Earth and its moon are different.

   _____

   _____

5. How do most scientists think the moon was formed?

   _____

   _____

Unifying Concepts and Processes

By 2020, NASA plans to be well underway with a project to build a space station and launch pad on the moon's surface, with a long-term goal of sending human beings to Mars. Why do you think launching spacecraft from the moon is a desirable alternative to launching them from Earth?

_____

_____

The Martian Question

probe: a spacecraft used to explore an object in outer space

microorganisms: living organisms that are too small to be seen without a microscope

inconclusive: having no final results or answers

extremophiles: organisms that have adapted to living in extreme temperatures, pressures, or chemical concentrations; they are usually single-celled organisms

thermal vents: openings in Earth, usually undersea, that emit hot water and minerals

In 1984, a meteorite was found in Antarctica that is thought to have come originally from Mars. The meteorite is estimated to be 4.5 billion years old, and it contains what many believe is the first evidence of extraterrestrial life. Scientists investigating the meteorite discovered what they think are the fossilized remains of extremely tiny bacteria that made the trip from Mars to Earth. The meteor landed in Antarctica 13,000 years ago.

If life exists on Mars, what will it look like?

During the 1800s, powerful new telescopes allowed astronomers to see Mars with more clarity than had ever before been possible. They discovered icecaps similar to Earth's covering each of the planet's poles. Martian days turned out to be nearly identical to Earth's. The planet also tilts on its axis, like Earth, to create a year of seasons. These similarities to our planet were interesting, but it was the canals that appeared to criss-cross the planet's surface that really got the scientists excited.

Around 1900, astronomer Percival Lowell published several books arguing that the canals proved the existence of an advanced Martian society. Before Lowell had even written his first book, though, most astronomers knew that the canals were an optical illusion. Spectrographs of the Martian atmosphere showed that it contains almost no water or oxygen—the two substances considered essential for life. Lowell's reputation suffered among scientists, but the public enjoyed his books.

In the 1960s, *Mariner 4* orbited Mars and returned photographs showing a desolate, dry landscape. The spacecraft's instruments also determined that Mars had no magnetic field, so dangerous levels of ultraviolet radiation bombarded the surface. The planet's atmospheric pressure was also too low for liquid water to exist on the planet's surface.

What about underground, though? Single-celled organisms, like bacteria, might be able to survive somewhere below the surface. The *Viking* missions of the 1970s landed a **probe** on Mars. The probe conducted experiments to see whether or not **microorganisms** lived in the planet's soil. The probe scooped up soil samples and then analyzed them for chemicals that a living organism would produce as waste. The results were **inconclusive**.

Since then, the search for Martian life has changed directions. Scientists are now trying to find out if liquid water ever existed on the planet's surface. Even if life doesn't exist on Mars today, showing that life once existed there could lead to new ideas about how life arose here on Earth, too.

Scientists also study life-forms here on Earth called **extremophiles**. These unusual organisms survive in conditions that no one thought could support life. Extremophiles have been found in the boiling waters of **thermal vents**, in rocks buried a mile underground, and in the ice of Antarctica. They may be the key to what life beyond Earth looks like.

Circle the letter of the best answer to each question below.

1. Both Mars and Earth

    a. have water.

    b. tilt on their axes.

    c. have atmospheres.

    d. All of the above

2. The Martian canals turned out to be

    a. filled with ice.

    b. optical illusions.

    c. canyons.

    d. marks left behind by NASA spacecraft.

3. The results of *Viking's* experiments

    a. proved that life couldn't exist in the Martian soil.

    b. proved that living organisms would be found only at the poles.

    c. couldn't be used to determine whether life did or did not exist on Mars.

    d. showed that if life did exist on Mars, it would have to exist deep underground.

Write your answers on the lines below.

4. Why would bacteria in a meteorite from Mars help explain how life arose on Earth?

    _____

    _____

5. Why are extremophiles important in studying the possibility of life on other planets?

    _____

What's Next?

NASA's *Phoenix* spacecraft landed on the Martian surface in May of 2008. The craft landed near Mars's north pole and analyzed the frozen water found there. Do some research to learn more about the *Phoenix* mission, and what scientists learned about the possibilities of life on Mars.

Review

Circle the letter of the best answer to each question below.

1. Which of the following is not a common effect of El Niños?

   a. droughts in Southern California

   b. flooding in Peru

   c. droughts in Indonesia

   d. warmer than usual waters along the western coastlines of the Americas

2. Which of these statements is true?

   a. All rocks are minerals.

   b. All minerals are rocks.

   c. All rocks are crystals.

   d. All minerals are crystals.

3. What characteristics of extremophiles make them valuable examples of what life might be like on another planet?

   a. They survive in conditions that are much too harsh for most other life on Earth.

   b. They have been found living on satellites that orbit Earth.

   c. Their fossilized remains have been found in meteorites.

   d. The *Viking* lander found evidence of their chemical waste in Martian soil.

Use the words in the box to complete the sentences below.

biological	plate tectonics	symmetrical	celestial	saturated	topographical

4. The movement of segments of Earth's crust, known as _____, may be one of the causes of ice ages.

5. _____ maps show terrain and ocean depths in three dimensions.

6. When the ground is completely filled with water, it is _____.

7. _____ weathering can be caused by plant roots growing in the cracks of a rock.

8. A crystal's structure consists of a repeated pattern of _____ solids.

9. The largest gravitationally-bound _____ objects are clusters.

Write your answers on the lines below.

10. Describe what an ice age is, including how long it lasts and the phases it goes through.

_____

_____

11. Are avalanches more likely to occur on steep or gentle, gradual inclines? Explain.

_____

_____

12. Give two examples of avalanche triggers.

_____   _____

13. Explain how groundwater is a part of the water cycle.

_____

_____

14. How can the water supply in an aquifer get polluted by chemicals?

_____

15. What is the difference between mechanical and chemical weathering?

_____

_____

16. Debris that was left over after the sun formed came together to form planets and other objects in the solar system because of _____.

17. What do most of today's scientists think is the origin of Earth's moon?

_____

18. Why are scientists searching for evidence of liquid water on Mars?

_____

Lesson 5.1 Copycats

cloning: creating an exact copy of an organism

replicas: duplicates; exact copies

genetic modification: the changing of an organism by the introduction of genes it does not naturally possess

Cloning could be used to increase populations of endangered animals. Even extinct animals might be cloned if a complete, undamaged sample of the animal's DNA was found. A similar animal, a sort of foster parent, would need to be available so that the embryo could be implanted in it. For this reason, it wouldn't be possible to clone dinosaurs, even if DNA could be located.

One problem with cloning animals is that it would reduce genetic diversity. In nature, the different members of a species have different strengths, which can make the population stronger. Identical, cloned animals could be more vulnerable to being wiped out by a disease or a change in environment.

What use does science have for clones?

Although it has made quite a stir and created a lot of controversy, **cloning** is nothing new. To clone something is to create an exact copy of it. Identical twins are genetically exactly the same, but they aren't clones because one twin wasn't created from the other. Some single-celled bacteria reproduce by cloning, meaning that a cell duplicates its DNA, and the offspring are exact **replicas** of the parent organism. Even some plants reproduce by cloning.

This type of natural cloning isn't what all the controversy is about, however. For years, scientists around the world have been experimenting with ways in which animals can be cloned using the cells of an adult animal. When two parent animals reproduce under normal conditions, the offspring will have a random mixture of genes from each parent. Cloning takes away the element of chance. A clone has only one parent, and thus the exact same set of genes as that parent.

Advances in technology have given scientists the ability to determine which traits they want a generation of plants or animals to possess—a process called **genetic modification**. The advantage of this is that crops can be produced that are resistant to certain diseases or drought. Vegetables may grow especially large or have a long shelf. A breed of cow may produce extra-large quantities of milk. Cloning a genetically-modified organism would allow scientists to create large quantities of desirable animals that could save farmers and consumers lots of money.

In 1996, the first successfully cloned mammal, a sheep named *Dolly*, was born. Since that time, about a dozen other species of animals, including deer, horses, pigs, and cats, have been cloned. These animals tend to have health problems, though, and seldom reach old age.

The cloning of animals has also raised all sorts of ethical and religious questions. Is it morally okay to duplicate a living creature? If animals can be cloned, will human beings be next? What sorts of problems could this create? For example, could human beings be created to have certain desirable characteristics, such as physical beauty or exceptional athletic ability? Currently, many countries have a ban on cloning human beings because of moral concerns and worries that serious defects could result. It's likely, though, that someday there will be human clones. It may not occur in our lifetimes, but it will present future generations with many interesting issues.

NAME _____

Use the words in the box to complete the sentences below.

| controversial | DNA | characteristics | genetic diversity |

1. Two organisms that are exactly the same share the same _____.

2. _____ means that animals within a population have a variety of strengths.

3. Because of the many ethical issues that surround cloning, it is a _____ subject.

4. Genetically modified animals often possess _____ that farmers find valuable.

Write your answers on the lines below.

5. How are identical twins different from a clone and its parent? How are they similar?

_____

_____

6. What two main conditions are necessary for an extinct animal to be cloned?

_____

7. In theory, which would be more likely to be cloned—a prehistoric relative of the tiger or a brontosaurus? Explain your answer.

_____

8. How does genetic diversity benefit a population of animals?

_____

_____

9. What is genetic modification, and how does it play a role in the cloning of animals?

_____

Unifying Concepts and Processes

Are cloned animals really exactly like? If a human being were cloned, would he or she be an exact replica of the parent who provided the DNA? Use what you know about heredity and environment (nature versus nurture) to form a detailed response.

_____

_____

Where Art and Science Meet

pigments: dry, colored substances from nature that are ground up and mixed with water, oil, or another base to create paints

digital technology: devices, such as computers, cameras, or musical instruments, that use digital code

medium: a material or technique used by an artist

printmaking: an artistic medium that involves making multiple copies of an image

etching: the process of creating images on a metal, glass, or other type of plate through the corrosive action of an acid

corrosive: having the power to wear away by chemical action

lithography: a printing process in which a plate is treated to retain ink in the areas of the image, while the nonimage areas are made to repel ink

viscosity: the resistance of a substance to flow

"Art is born of the observation and investigation of nature."
—Cicero, ancient Roman statesman and philosopher

How do scientific discoveries impact the world of art?

Artists have always relied on science and technology to provide them with new methods of expression. Painting, for example, started with the discovery of how to extract **pigments** from nature. Tools for carving wood and stone had to be invented before anyone could begin sculpting. **Digital technology** is one of the newest means of artistic expression.

In the history of art, photography is also a relatively new artistic **medium**. It's a form of **printmaking** that uses light-sensitive chemicals. The special properties of these substances were discovered only a couple of hundred years ago, but artists soon found ways to use them creatively. Chemistry plays an important role in other forms of printmaking as well. Here are two examples of how chemical properties are used by printers.

- **Etching** was discovered about 500 years ago. An artist uses **corrosive** chemicals to etch an image into a copper plate. First, the plate is covered with a thin layer of asphalt. Then, using a sharp tool, an image is scratched into the asphalt. Anywhere a line has been made exposes the copper underneath the asphalt. The plate is submerged in a vat of strong acid, and the exposed copper gets eaten away. After a while, the plate is lifted out of the vat, the acid is rinsed off, and the asphalt is removed. The copper plate now has etched lines that echo the image that had been scratched into the asphalt. The plate is covered in ink and then wiped off, but ink remains in the etched lines. Wet paper pressed against the plate absorbs the remaining ink, and the printing process is complete.

- **Lithography** was invented around 1800. It works because of **viscosity**, or the different "thicknesses" liquids have. Viscosity is the reason that oil and water don't mix. First, an image is drawn onto a lithographic plate, usually made of limestone or aluminum. Then, a salt solution is spread across the plate. This solution gets absorbed into the plate wherever the image doesn't block it. Next, the image is wiped away and the plate is moistened with water. The water is drawn to the salty areas and away from those areas that had been protected by the image. Then, an oil-based ink is rolled across the plate. Oil and water don't mix, so the ink only sticks to the dry areas that were created by the original image. Paper pressed against the plate picks up the ink, and the printing process is complete.

Circle the letter of the best answer to each question below.

1. A copper plate that has been etched

    a. uses acid-based inks.

    b. holds ink in thin grooves that were eaten into its surface.

    c. can print only onto acid-free paper.

    d. uses asphalt instead of ink to print an image.

2. Viscosity refers to

    a. the plates used in the lithographic printing process.

    b. the acid used to etch copper plates.

    c. how easily a liquid flows.

    d. how quickly a digital device processes information.

Write your answers on the lines below.

3. What do you think would happen if you removed the copper plate from the acid bath too soon?

    _____

4. Choose any artistic medium, and then describe how a technology or scientific discovery not already mentioned in this selection influences it or makes it possible.

    _____

    _____

5. Do you think creativity is important in science as well as art? Why or why not?

    _____

    _____

What's Next?

In 2000, artist Eduardo Kac asked a laboratory to combine the genes of a rabbit with genes from a type of glowing jellyfish. Alba was the result—a genetically-modified rabbit that glows green in the dark. Many people were offended by this work and considered it to be cruel. Others believed it was a new, creative form of artistic expression using cutting-edge scientific research. What do you think?

Buildings in the Clouds

reinforced concrete: cement powder, sand or gravel, and water poured around a steel grid of bars

wind tunnels: scientifically controlled wind environments

bedrock: solid rock that lies below the soil and the loose rocks near Earth's surface

Taipei 101 in Taiwan is currently the world's tallest skyscraper. However, once completed, Burj Dubai in Dubai, United Arab Emirates, will surpass Taipei 101.

"Architecture is the alphabet of giants; it is the largest set of symbols ever made to meet the eyes of men. A tower stands up like a sort of simplified statue, of much more than heroic size."
—Gilbert Chesterton, writer and poet

To make the vertical concrete supports, builders put steel rods into wooden forms and then pour concrete around the steel. A climbing jack lifts the form, and builders add more rods and concrete to add height.

How are the world's tallest buildings constructed?

Towers are some of the most fascinating buildings in architecture. People have been constructing them since ancient times, but until the late 1800s, towers were made of stone. The walls had to be very thick to hold the weight of the building and its contents. Windows were small so they wouldn't weaken the structure, and the rooms were cramped and dark.

In the 1800s, American factories started mass-producing iron and steel, and railroads made these materials more readily available. People found that they could build with steel instead of stone, and that buildings could be taller because steel is lighter. In 1857, the first passenger elevator was installed, and the first skyscrapers were built by the end of that century.

Each skyscraper is one-of-a-kind, but all have a skeleton made of steel or **reinforced concrete**, a central support tube, or both. In some buildings, the outside walls hang like curtains on the frame and serve only to seal the building from the weather. In other buildings, the outside walls also support the building, connecting horizontally to the core and to each other. The John Hancock Building in Chicago and the former Twin Towers of the World Trade Center are examples of this type of construction.

Skyscrapers need to be strong enough to support the weight of the building and everything inside it, but they must also be able to withstand heavy winds, a major stress on the building. Architects must plan for huge windstorms, such as hurricanes and tornadoes. By building models of their designs and putting them in **wind tunnels**, they can accurately gauge the strength of the full-sized buildings.

Before a skyscraper can be built, workers have to dig a deep hole into the **bedrock** that is up to 200 feet beneath the soil. Poles made of steel or reinforced concrete are anchored in the rock. Then, concrete is poured for the floor, and the construction begins. Cranes lift the steel girders, which are welded into place. The vertical beams support the weight of the building and the horizontal beams hold it together.

Different stages of construction happen at the same time. After the core or supports are a few stories high, the bottom floors are added. Workers finish the insides of the lower floors while upper floors are built. As the building grows, cranes move to the upper floors, all the way to the top, changing the skyline as a new skyscraper takes its place in the city.

Circle the letter of the best answer to the question below.

1. Why did people begin building towers of steel rather than stone?

   a. The supply of stone was beginning to run out.

   b. Steel was lighter so the buildings could be taller.

   c. Railroads made materials more widely available.

   d. Both b and c

Write your answers on the lines below.

2. Give two examples of advances in technology that made the construction of modern skyscrapers possible.

   _____

   _____

3. Explain how the construction of the John Hancock building is different from that of a skyscraper in which the walls only hang over the frame or skeleton of the building.

   _____

   _____

4. How are buildings like skyscrapers anchored in the ground?

   _____

5. What weather phenomenon places a great deal of stress on skyscrapers? How can architects and engineers be sure the buildings can withstand these forces?

   _____

   _____

6. Why do you think stone was a popular building material for towers before steel and iron became available?

   _____

   _____

refracts: alters light waves from moving in their natural, straight path

convex: having a surface that is curved outward

converge: to approach or meet at the same intersecting point

focal point: the point where light waves that have passed through a lens converge

prisms: clear, solid forms that break up white light into the separate wavelengths of color that it contains

concave: having a surface that is curved inward

Patriot, politician, and inventor Benjamin Franklin designed the first bifocals. The top half of these lenses is concave to help the wearer see distant objects more clearly. The bottom half of a bifocal lens is convex to help bring nearby objects into focus.

Most lenses today are made of special plastics. The way these lenses refract light is determined by their chemical properties and not their overall thickness or shape.

Who invented eyeglasses?

Lenses are used in devices like microscopes, cameras, and lasers, but for many people, the lenses they know best sit right in front of their faces. A lens **refracts** light waves, and eyeglasses use this optical property to help people see better.

Ancient Greek writings from 2,000 years ago referred to lenses being used to start fires, and for several centuries, that was their main use. These early lenses were **convex**, which means their sides curved outward. Light waves passing through a convex lens refract inward, and eventually they **converge** at a singular **focal point** on the other side. When sunlight passes through a convex lens, its heat energy is also focused into a single, hot spot that can ignite flammable materials.

Around A.D. 1000, the Islamic scientist Alhazen published his *Book of Optics*. It contained his groundbreaking observations about the properties of light, lenses, and **prisms**. Alhazen also correctly described for the first time how the human eye works. The front of the eyeball has an opening that's covered by a convex lens. Light waves pass through this lens and focus images of the world onto the back of the eyeball, where a light-sensitive area, called the *retina*, is found. The optic nerve carries this image to the brain, and we see the world that surrounds us.

Although the magnifying properties of convex lenses were discovered earlier, the first eyeglasses weren't invented until around 1280 in Italy. These lenses helped correct hyperopia, or farsightedness. People with hyperopia have trouble seeing things nearby. Their focal point ends up falling somewhere beyond the back of the eyeball. The convex lenses in a pair of eyeglasses help the light waves converge sooner so the focal point lands where it should.

Concave lenses weren't invented until a couple of hundred years later. Their sides curve inward, and they spread light waves apart instead of causing them to converge. Eyeglasses with concave lenses correct myopia, or nearsightedness. The lens in the eye of a person with myopia causes the light waves to converge too soon and land in front of the retina. Eyeglasses with concave lenses spread the light waves a bit. The focal point is pushed backward so that it falls directly onto the retina, and distant objects become clear.

Circle the letter of the best answer to each question below.

1. Where were eyeglasses first invented?

   a. Ancient Greece

   b. Ancient Islam

   c. Italy

   d. The selection did not say.

2. A lens with sides that curve inward is

   a. convex.

   b. concave.

   c. focal.

   d. prismatic.

3. The light-sensitive area at the back of the eye is the

   a. pupil.

   b. lens.

   c. retina.

   d. optic nerve.

Write your answers on the lines below.

4. Using vocabulary from the selection, explain in detail how a lens corrects myopia.

   _____

   _____

   _____

5. Explain how a prism is different from a lens.

   _____

   _____

Unifying Concepts and Properties

Do you think a mirror refracts light? Why or why not?

   _____

The Instruments of Weather Science

meteorologist: a scientist who makes short-term weather predictions

climatologist: a scientist who studies long-term weather effects on climates

hygrometers: instruments that measure humidity

barometer: an instrument that measures atmospheric pressure

sea level: level of the ocean's surface, used as a reference point for determining an area's elevation

Climate is the long-term weather conditions in a particular area. The amounts of snow or rain, the average temperatures, and average wind speeds are all factors taken into consideration.

Have you ever noticed your hair get curly and wild on a hot, sticky day? Humidity can change the length of your hair by as much as 3%. In fact, scientists used hygrometers with strands of human hair from 1783 until the 1960s to measure humidity.

How can scientists predict the future?

If you want to know the forecast for tomorrow's weather, ask a **meteorologist**. If you want to know what the weather will be like a 100 years from now, you need to ask a **climatologist**. Meteorologists and climatologists look at weather in different ways, but they use many of the same tools.

Although temperature can be measured in a number of different ways, the traditional bulb thermometer is still the most common device. These thermometers are thin tubes containing liquids, like mercury or alcohol, which are very sensitive to slight changes in heat, and readily expand or contract with each tiny variation in temperature.

Temperature can also be measured with electronic sensors that detect the amount of infrared radiation, or heat, an object emits. This is how some satellites read Earth's temperatures on the surface or in the atmosphere.

Hygrometers measure the amount of humidity, or water vapor, in the air. The most common version of this device uses two thermometers—one with a dry bulb and one that's wet. As the moisture on the wet thermometer evaporates, it carries heat with it. How much moisture evaporates—and therefore how much the temperature drops—depends on how humid the surrounding air is. The temperature difference between the two thermometers is used to calculate the percent of water vapor in the air.

A **barometer** measures atmospheric pressure, or the weight of the air. Earth's atmosphere contains miles and miles of air molecules affected by gravity. Atmospheric pressure changes all the time depending on the temperature and how high an area is above **sea level**. Some barometers contain mercury that rises or drops inside tubes. These tubes are vacuums with open ends sitting in dishes of mercury. An increase in pressure pushes down on the mercury's surface in the dish and forces mercury up into the tube. When pressure drops, the reverse happens, and the mercury level inside the tube falls. A fall in air pressure is important when predicting the weather because it usually means a storm is on the way.

One tool climatologists—but not meteorologists—use is a borer. It can remove long, cylindrical pieces of wood from trees. In climates with changing seasons, trees form new rings each year. During years with mild weather, a long growing season, and plenty of rain, trees grow wider rings. Dry years produce narrow rings. Climatologists can look at these samples and create a year-by-year history of climates spanning centuries.

Circle the letter of the best answer to each question below.

1. Which of the following is not true of hygrometers?

   a. They work only at sea level.

   b. They measure humidity.

   c. They use thermometers.

   d. They might contain mercury.

2. When temperatures rise, the mercury or alcohol in a thermometer also rises because

   a. its molecules have more energy.

   b. heat creates additional alcohol or mercury that fills the tube.

   c. the rising temperatures create a vacuum that draws these substances upward.

   d. the tube contracts and becomes thinner, which forces the liquids upward.

Write your answers on the lines below.

3. How is climatology different from meteorology? How are the two fields similar?

   _____

   _____

4. Explain how a hygrometer works.

   _____

   _____

5. Is barometric pressure higher or lower at sea level compared to the top of a mountain? Explain your answer.

   _____

   _____

Unifying Concepts and Processes

Water placed into a vacuum will begin to boil at normal room temperatures. Mercury is also a liquid. Why doesn't it boil in the vacuum tube of a barometer?

   _____

   _____

The Power of Music

amplified: made louder or more powerful

electromagnetism: the physics of electromagnetic forces

fluctuations: variations or changes

induce: to produce, cause, or bring about, especially in relation to electrical currents

electrical amplifier: a device that converts a small electric signal into a larger one

Feedback can be a painful, screeching sound when it gets out of control, but some musicians use it as an additional element in their music. Feedback happens when the sounds coming from a speaker cause the guitar's strings to vibrate. These vibrations go to the amplifier, exit the speaker, hit the strings, and cause them to vibrate even more powerfully. The vibrations travel this loop until the sound waves build into a high-pitched squeal.

Amplification became necessary in the Big Band era because the large brass sections were drowning out the guitarists.

How do electric guitars produce such loud sounds?

The crowd roars as the band jogs onstage. With one swipe across six steel strings, the guitarist drowns out an entire stadium of screaming people with the sound coming from a single guitar. How did the strings' vibrations turn into such powerful sound waves?

The strings of an acoustic guitar are stretched across a round opening in the guitar's body. The vibrating strings create sound waves that enter this hole, bounce around inside the deep, hollow space, and become **amplified**. The body of an electric guitar is flat and solid, though. When it's not plugged into an amplifier, the strings sound quiet and muffled when they're plucked.

Electric guitars produce their sound based on properties of **electromagnetism**. During the early 1800s, Michael Faraday showed how electricity and magnetism were related. He discovered that **fluctuations**, or changes, in a magnetic field caused an electrical current to flow through a wire. When he reversed the experiment, he showed that an electrical current could also produce a magnetic field. Electricity and magnetism are now viewed as a single force called *electromagnetism*.

Lying below each string of an electric guitar is a magnet surrounded by a coil of wire, called a *pickup*. The magnetic field of one object can often create a magnetic field in another object, especially when the objects are metal. The guitar's steel strings become magnetized by the magnets lying below them, and the two magnetic fields are connected at their poles.

When a guitarist plucks a string, it begins to vibrate, and the vibrations cause both magnetic fields to fluctuate. As Faraday demonstrated, a fluctuating magnetic field will **induce** an electrical current. Inside the guitar, the changing magnetic field causes electrons to begin moving through the coil of wire that surrounds the magnet.

The coils are connected to electrical wires that carry the current out of the guitar and through a cord that's connected to an **electrical amplifier**. The amplifier boosts the current's power and sends it on to a speaker.

The speakers do everything in reverse. The electrical current is used to create a fluctuating magnetic field, and this changing field causes magnets to vibrate. The magnets are attached to paper cones, and the vibrating cones send sound waves through the air. Powerful electrical currents and huge speakers can create incredibly loud sounds—loud enough to entertain a stadium filled with music lovers!

NAME _____

Circle the letter of the best answer to each question below.

1. The steel strings on an electric guitar are

   a. magnetized.

   b. electrified.

   c. Both a and b

   d. Neither a nor b

2. What does an electrical amplifier do?

   a. It provides electrical power for the guitar.

   b. It creates sound waves.

   c. It makes an electrical current more powerful.

   d. All of the above

3. Fluctuations in a magnetic field will

   a. produce more powerful magnetic energy.

   b. cause another object to become magnetized.

   c. transmit sound waves through space.

   d. induce an electrical current in a wire.

4. What is a pickup?

   a. a cord that connects a guitar to an amplifier

   b. a magnet surrounded by a coil of wire

   c. a device used to pluck or strum guitar strings

   d. an opening in an acoustic guitar's body

Write your answers on the lines below.

5. Do electric guitars need to be plugged into electrical outlets? Explain your answer.

   _____

   _____

6. Briefly describe how speakers produce sound.

   _____

   _____

The Future's Calling

cellular network: a large radio communication system with several transmitting towers that each covers a smaller area, called a *cell*

signals: sounds, images, or other messages that are sent or received using electrical currents, radio waves, light, or other means

landlines: a wire or cable used to carry telephone signals

FCC: the Federal Communications Commission; a government agency that monitors and controls all communication signals sent and received in the United States

After the telephone was invented, nearly 100 years passed before the first billion people had access to phones. After cell phones became available, though, it took only ten years for another billion people to get access.

What do cells have to do with cell phones?

Almost anywhere you go, there's a good chance you'll hear the ring of someone's cell phone. Just 20 years ago, mobile phones were still rare. They were much bigger than today's cell phones, and they usually were installed inside cars. As technology improved, and a worldwide **cellular network** was established, cell phones became smaller and more convenient.

Mobile phones combine radio technology with telephone technology. The phone itself is a two-way radio. When you make a call, radio waves carrying coded information are transmitted and received by the phone. These **signals** travel back and forth between your phone and a nearby cell tower. At the base of the tower is equipment that connects you to the larger phone system of **landlines** and satellites—the global communications network that carries messages all over the world.

Landlines transmit sound by encoding information into electrical currents. Sound waves entering the phone's receiver cause fluctuations in an electrical current. The altered current travels through wires to someone's phone at the other end. The information carried by the electrical current is turned back into sound waves by a speaker in the phone receiver.

Radios don't need wires because they use electromagnetic energy waves to send and receive information. A transmitter changes sound waves into signals that are encoded in a radio wave. A radio receiver reads the altered radio wave and changes the information back into sound.

Radios and telephones were both invented in the late 1800s. Radios were mobile from the start—batteries could always provide the power they needed. Telephones needed wires to transmit their messages.

The idea of creating a radio that could connect with the phone system began in the1940s. The **FCC** designated a small portion of the electromagnetic spectrum for this technology, but it quickly became obvious that this portion was much too small. If more than a few dozen people tried to use radiophones at once, the signals would interfere with each other.

This problem led to the creation of cellular technology. Instead of having one big, powerful tower covering a large area, each tower covers only one small area, called a *cell*. The limited number of radio frequencies set aside for radiophones can be reused from cell to cell. As long as there are plenty of towers around, there's plenty of signal space to handle everyone's calls.

Circle the letter of the best answer to the question below.

1. In the term *cell phone*, "cell" refers to

    a. the battery that powers the phone.

    b. the equipment used to change radio waves to electrical signals.

    c. the area covered by a radio tower.

    d. the device in the phone that transmits radio signals.

Write your answers on the lines below.

2. A cellular network consists of many radio-antennae towers, but it's much more efficient than a mobile phone system that uses only one powerful tower. Why?

    _____

    _____

    _____

3. Cellular networks are less expensive to build than phone systems that rely on landlines. Why do you think that is?

    _____

    _____

Unifying Concepts and Processes

In the last 20 years, improvements in computer technology have meant that increasingly smaller pieces of equipment are able to process information more quickly. How do you think these improvements in computer technology have affected cell phones?

_____

_____

What's Next?

A radio station's number, like 1020 AM or 99.5 FM, refers to the specific frequency that the station uses for broadcasting. Each different type of radio communication uses a set range of frequencies in the spectrum. Which do you think are longer—AM or FM radio wavelengths? What about television broadcasts? Find a chart showing the different ranges of radio wavelengths and their uses.

network: computers connected to share information

routers: intermediate computers that connect multiple networks

GUIs: Graphical User Interfaces, pronounced *goo ees*; easy-to-use pictures and symbols that can be clicked on in order to give the computer instructions

software: a program that allows a computer to perform a specific task

With the growth of the Internet came the first virus in 1988. It was called the *Internet Worm*, and it temporarily shut down about 10% of the world's Internet servers. By 2000, programmers created self-replicating viruses like "Love Bug" and "Stages." These viruses hack into the user's e-mail address book and forward the virus to everyone listed in it. Computer viruses are created by programmers and are spread as pranks or vandalism, or for financial gain.

How did the Internet begin?

Since the mid-1990s, the Internet has become an important part of our daily lives. It allows us to communicate with friends and family, read a menu for a restaurant in Paris, or view images taken by the *Pathfinder* on Mars. With the Internet, people can work while on the road or at home and still be connected with a main office.

The Internet is a series of interconnected computers linked by telephone, fiber optics, satellite, and cable. E-mail and the World Wide Web are software programs used on the Internet.

While it may seem that the Internet is a recent development, its origins are during the Cold War. In 1969, the U.S. Department of Defense developed an early form of the Internet with a computer **network** known as ARPANET. University and government researchers needed to quickly share information from various locations across the country. Even more importantly, the government believed the military needed a secondary communication system in case a nuclear attack destroyed phone lines. Prior to this, computers could "talk" to each other, but interaction was limited because they had to be physically connected. ARPANET allowed a user to send packets of information via **routers** to their final destination.

The early Internet looked very different from what we use today. It lacked **GUIs**, graphics, and Web pages. It primarily consisted of e-mails, mailing lists, and some simple games. By 1985, home computers were beginning to become more affordable. Companies began to offer the Internet to home users, with access to bulletin boards, e-mail, and news.

In 1991, Tim Berners-Lee, a researcher in a physics laboratory, developed the building blocks of the World Wide Web. To create Web pages, he wrote the **software** for the following programs: Universal Resource Locator (URL)—used to give Web page locations, Hypertext Transfer Protocol (HTTP)—used to process the information, Hypertext Markup Language (HTML)—used to create Web pages, and hyperlinks—used to link a word in an article to a different article or Web site.

By 1996, 45 million people were using the Internet with 30 million users in North America. Today, more than one billion people use the Internet, with more than half the users living in Asia or North America. With the ability to easily connect with someone on the other side of the globe, the Internet has forever changed our relationship with the world around us.

Circle the letter of the best answer to each question below.

1. Which of the following is an example of a URL?

    a. Internet graphics

    b. www.funwithscience.org

    c. Love Bug

    d. ARAPNET

2. How were early versions of the Internet different than the Internet of today?

    a. They didn't have Web pages.

    b. They didn't have e-mail.

    c. They didn't have games.

    d. Both a and b

Write your answers on the lines below.

3. Explain why ARPANET was developed.

    _____

    _____

4. How was ARPANET different from the ways in which earlier computers had communicated?

    _____

5. How do you think the affordability of computers influenced the development of the Internet?

    _____

6. What is one way computer viruses can spread?

    _____

7. How do computers around the world link to the Internet?

    _____

8. As you read a Web page about hurricanes, you notice that tornadoes are mentioned. The word *tornadoes* appears in a different color. If you click on it, you will be directed to a page with more

    information about tornadoes. This is an example of a _____.

isotope: one of two or more atoms that have equal numbers of protons but different numbers of neutrons

chain reaction: a process in which the results of one event trigger another similar event, which then triggers another similar event, and so on

fission: splitting of an unstable nucleus into two or more nuclei

fusion: combining two or more nuclei into a single, heavier nucleus

turbine: machine that uses the movement of a gas or liquid to turn a rotor

The Manhattan Project ran from 1941 through 1945. It involved many of the world's top physicists and more than 100,000 people working in about a dozen facilities scattered across the United States.

Hydrogen bombs combine fission and fusion technology to create weapons that are hundreds of times more powerful than the bombs dropped on Japan in 1945.

Will fusion be our main source of energy someday?

In the 1930s, scientists shot an extra neutron into the unstable nucleus of a uranium-235 **isotope**. One more particle was just too much for a nucleus that was already overstuffed with 143 neutrons. It split apart and formed two new atoms—a barium isotope and a krypton isotope. Some of the neutrons flew off by themselves, though, and bombarded the nuclei of other, nearby uranium-235 isotopes. These isotopes split apart as well and produced more loose neutrons, which flew off and split more isotopes, and so on. This **chain reaction** released an enormous amount of energy—millions of times greater than an equal amount of gasoline or coal could ever produce. Human beings had just discovered nuclear **fission**.

This new technology was quickly put to use in atomic weaponry. American leaders were concerned that Nazi Germany would harness the power of nuclear fission for a bomb. The Manhattan Project was created to develop an atomic weapon before the Nazis did.

The devastating explosion of a nuclear weapon is produced by an uncontrolled chain reaction. Once the war ended, scientists learned to control the reaction so that nuclear energy could be used more productively. Today, nuclear power plants provide about 20 percent of America's electricity.

While scientists were researching the power of fission, they were also investigating the power of **fusion**. When two nuclei are forced together, they combine to form one new, heavier nucleus. Like fission, fusion also releases enormous amounts of energy. It's how stars create their light and heat. Inside the sun, hydrogen atoms are fused together to form helium atoms.

A fusion reactor would create power in a way similar to the fission reactors in use today. The reaction heats water and creates steam pressure, which then turns a **turbine** and generates electricity. A fusion reactor would be safer, though. It doesn't hold much fuel, so if an accident did occur, the fuel would burn up in a minute or so. Fusion also doesn't produce highly radioactive waste that will remain dangerous for thousands of years.

A practical fusion reactor hasn't been developed yet, but scientists still hope that day will come. It takes a tremendous amount of energy to fuse two nuclei. An environment similar to the sun's interior has to be created. Once the first nuclei are fused, enough energy is produced to create a fusion chain reaction, with plenty of energy left over to generate electricity.

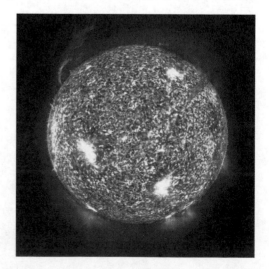

Circle the letter of the best answer to each question below.

1. A fission chain reaction is

    a. atoms crashing into each other.

    b. nuclei coming together to release energy.

    c. neutrons smashing into the nuclei of isotopes.

    d. nuclear energy moving a turbine.

2. Uranium-235 is _____ used in nuclear reactions.

    a. an isotope

    b. a neutron

    c. a fission

    d. a type of hydrogen

3. The sun is a giant fusion reactor that changes

    a. uranium into hydrogen.

    b. uranium into barium and krypton.

    c. uranium into uranium-235.

    d. hydrogen into helium.

Write your answers on the lines below.

4. Why haven't scientists built a practical fusion reactor yet?

    _____

5. Explain how a fusion reactor would be similar to a fission reactor.

    _____

6. Why would fusion be a better alternative to fission as an energy source?

    _____

What's Next?

The largest fusion research lab in the world is JET, or the Joint European Torus, located in the United Kingdom. Their Web site contains the most comprehensive and up-to-date information available about this cutting-edge technology.

Review

NAME _____

Circle the letter of the best answer to each question below.

1. Which of the following instruments contains mercury?

    a. thermometer

    b. hygrometer

    c. barometer

    d. All of the above

2. The pickup in an electric guitar

    a. changes sound waves into magnetic waves.

    b. uses fluctuations in a magnetic field to create an electrical current.

    c. amplifies the electrical current created by the strings.

    d. vibrates when the strings are plucked.

3. Which of the following devices is most similar to a cell phone?

    a. a walkie-talkie

    b. a traditional, landline telephone

    c. a telegraph

    d. a two-way radio

4. What is the most common use of uranium-235 isotopes?

    a. They're light-sensitive chemicals that can be used to create photographic images.

    b. They're an expanding and contracting liquid that's used in hygrometers.

    c. Their nuclei are split to create energy in nuclear reactors.

    d. They easily lose electrons, so they are used for electrical currents in amplifiers.

Write **true** or **false** next to each statement below.

5. _____ In general, cloning creates stronger and healthier animals.

6. _____ Viscosity is the reason that oil and water don't mix.

7. _____ Concave lenses were used for years to start fires.

8. _____ A barometer measures the amount of humidity in the air.

9. _____ The Internet and the World Wide Web are the same thing.

10. _____ An acoustic guitar's sound is amplified because of the guitar's hollow body.

Write your answers on the lines below.

11. Why is cloning a controversial topic?

   _____

   _____

12. What is one benefit to cloning animals?

   _____

13. Explain both the chemical and physical changes that occur when copper is etched.

   _____

   _____

14. How did the railroad industry have an impact on the construction of skyscrapers?

   _____

15. How are wind tunnels used in the creation of skyscrapers?

   _____

16. Explain the difference in shape between a concave and convex lens and the effect each has on light waves.

   _____

   _____

17. What form of electromagnetism do satellites detect to measure temperatures on Earth?

   _____

18. Explain how the Internet is a collaborative invention.

   _____

19. After dialing a number on a cell phone, where is the first place the signal travels to?

   _____

20. Explain the difference between fission and fusion.

   _____

Lesson 6.1   Say Cheese

plaque: a sticky, clear film that forms on the teeth

tartar: also called *calculus*; hardened plaque found on the teeth

Don't forget to brush your tongue each time you brush your teeth. Bacteria that live on your tongue can contribute to bad breath, also known as *halitosis*.

It's fine to have an occasional sweet treat—just brush your teeth afterward, or at least rinse your mouth with water. Try to avoid soda and other sugary drinks. If you do have one, use a straw so that the sticky liquid has less contact with your teeth, and rinse with water or brush your teeth when you're done.

Chewing sugar-free gum can actually be good for dental health. It keeps the saliva flowing, which washes away the acid on your teeth.

What's the best way to keep your pearly whites clean and healthy?

As a small child, you had a set of only 20 teeth until your permanent or adult teeth came in. Today, you have 32 teeth that need to last you a lifetime. Taking good care of your teeth is simple once you establish good habits.

Plaque is a sticky, clear film that builds up on your teeth. If you've ever forgotten to brush, you know just how it feels in your mouth. Not only can plaque cause bad breath, it can also lead to cavities. When you eat food that contains sugar and starches, plaque forms on your teeth. Bacteria in your mouth digests the plaque to form an acid that eats away at your enamel—the hard, protective coating on your teeth. When this happens repeatedly, the enamel breaks down and the tooth decays.

Cavities aren't the only damage that plaque causes, either. Over time, plaque that remains on the teeth hardens into **tartar**. Tartar makes it more difficult for you to properly clean your teeth. It can also lead to gingivitis, a form of gum disease, in which the gums are painful, irritated, and may bleed. This can be more than just an annoyance. Studies have found that poor dental health is actually considered a strong risk factor for heart disease.

Flossing is as important as brushing because it removes food and plaque from the spaces in between your teeth where the toothbrush can't reach. Flossing also strengthens your gums and helps keep them healthy.

Eating well is important to the health of your teeth, just as it is for the rest of your body. Foods rich in calcium, such as dairy products, help build healthy teeth and bones, where 99% of the body's calcium is found. Vitamin D is also essential, because it allows the body to absorb calcium. It's found in fortified foods, like milk, but it doesn't occur naturally in most foods. Luckily, the body can manufacture Vitamin D itself through exposure to ultraviolet sunlight for just a few minutes a day.

Even if you take all the proper measures to have a healthy mouth, regular visits to the dentist—approximately every six months—are still necessary. A dentist will clean your teeth, removing the tartar that builds up no matter how well you brush. He or she can also check for cavities and other

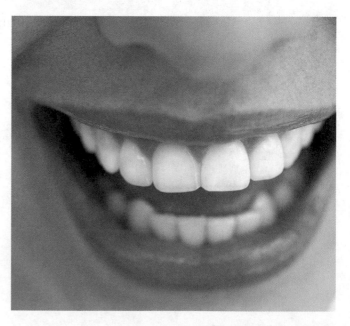

problems, like gum disease or oral cancer.

Write **true** or **false** next to each statement below.

1. _____ Human beings have more teeth as adults than they do as young children.

2. _____ Chewing any kind of gum is damaging to the health of your teeth.

3. _____ It's best to schedule a visit to the dentist once every two years.

4. _____ Brushing your tongue can help keep your breath smelling fresh.

5. _____ The human body can manufacture its own calcium and Vitamin D.

6. _____ Flossing can be a substitute for brushing your teeth.

7. _____ Plaque that is not removed from the teeth and hardens is called *tartar*.

8. _____ Gingivitis is a treatment that can prevent the formation of cavities.

Write your answers on the lines below.

9. Although it's best to avoid drinks that are high in sugar, what should you do if you have one?

_____

_____

10. Explain why both Vitamin D and calcium are necessary for the health of your teeth and bones.

_____

_____

11. What are two sources of Vitamin D?

_____

12. How do cavities form?

_____

_____

13. How does dental health relate to the health of other systems in the body?

_____

Brain Food

glucose: a form of sugar that travels through the bloodstream and provides fuel to cells

antioxidants: substances found in certain foods that can combat free radicals

free radicals: compounds that can harm living cells

Trans fatty acids are most often found in fast foods and prepackaged foods, like French fries, snack crackers, and cookies. Not only can they be harmful to brain functioning, they can also contribute to heart disease.

Some nutritious foods, like milk and fruits, contain simple carbs. Don't avoid them just because they don't have complex carbs. They have other health benefits that make them worth eating. Try to stick to whole fruits instead of fruit juices, and remember to choose low-fat milk, yogurt, and cheeses.

What's the best way to feed your brain?

Eating nutritious foods can help you stay fit and trim. Even more importantly, it can contribute to brain health. Many people don't realize that the foods they eat affect memory, mood, behavior, and thinking skills. By making certain foods a part of your diet, you can increase your brain power and help your brain achieve peak performance.

About two-thirds of the brain is composed of fats. Fatty acids make up a large part of the membranes of neurons—the nerve cells that transmit messages within the brain. Your body needs two types of essential fatty acids. Omega-3s can be found in cold-water fish, like salmon, trout, and sardines, as well as in nuts and avocados. Omega-6s are found in sunflower, corn, soy, and sesame oil, as well as in nuts, seeds, and **legumes**. The body can't manufacture these fatty acids, so you need to consume them regularly.

Amino acids, also important to brain health, are found in protein-rich foods like fish, meat, eggs, and dairy products. Your brain needs amino acids to form neurotransmitters—chemicals that can affect your moods and feelings. Neurotransmitters play a role in your ability to concentrate, feel motivated and alert, create memories, sleep well, and learn.

Just as a car needs gasoline to perform, your brain needs fuel provided by **glucose**. Have you ever skipped breakfast and found yourself unable to concentrate at school? Low blood sugar could have been responsible. Glucose is found in carbohydrates, but it's better to choose complex carbs than simple ones. Complex carbs are found in whole-grain breads, cereals, and pastas, as well as in legumes and some vegetables. They take your body longer to digest, so they release energy over a period of time. Soda and sugary foods contain simple carbs. A rush of sugar can make you briefly feel energized, but a few hours later you'll "crash" and feel even more tired.

Micronutrients, such as vitamins and minerals, are the final key to keeping your brain healthy and happy. **Antioxidants**, like vitamins E and C, are especially important in fighting **free radicals**, or harmful ions. Fruits and vegetables, seeds, nuts, whole grains, eggs, fish, lean meats, and dairy products are excellent sources of micronutrients.

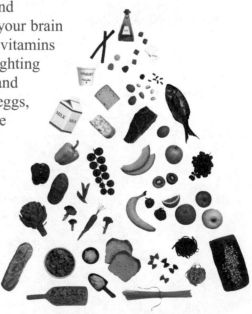

Eat a nutritious and varied diet, and you'll notice the effects in your ability to think clearly, learn quickly, remember things, and feel content. What could be more important than the health of your brain?

Circle the letter of the best answer to each question below.

1. In which of the following foods are trans fats most likely to be found?

   a. scrambled eggs

   b. a chicken sandwich

   c. potato chips

   d. mashed potatoes

2. Why is it important to eat foods that are rich sources of antioxidants?

   a. They turn the sugars in simple carbs into complex carbs.

   b. They help release glucose more slowly into your body.

   c. They protect your body's cells from micronutrients.

   d. They fight free radicals, which can damage the cells in your body.

Write your answers on the lines below.

3. Look at each meal listed below. Choose the meal that is a better choice for your brain, and list three reasons why.

   Meal A: a glass of grape juice, a hamburger on a white bun, a baked potato with full-fat sour cream and cheddar cheese, and a chocolate milkshake

   Meal B: a bowl of sliced strawberries, fish tacos on a whole-grain tortilla with shredded lettuce and tomato salsa, and low-fat yogurt with chopped nuts and dried fruit

   _____

   _____

4. Give examples of three foods that contain essential fatty acids.

   _____

5. Explain why it's wise to choose complex carbohydrates over simple ones, and give an example of each.

   _____

   _____

   _____

Looking for Alternatives

alternative medicine: any form of medical treatment used instead of traditional Western medicine

immune: able to resist a disease

philosophies: systems of ideas and beliefs

complementary medicine: the combined use of Western medicine and alternative medicine, utilizing the strengths of each

China has a written history of acupuncture that is more than 2,000 years old, but tiny stone needles have been found that are at least 4,000 years old. People later used gold, silver, and bronze needles. Today's acupuncture needles are made of surgical steel.

Yoga is a health philosophy that has been around for at least 5,000 years. It comes from an ancient civilization in what are now India and Pakistan. Yoga is more than just stretching exercises; it is a whole philosophy of breathing, relaxation, nutrition, and meditation.

The federal government does not test herbal medicine as it does prescription medicine, so consumers need to be careful.

What should people look for, or look out for, in natural healing?

Alternative medicine is treatment that is different from traditional Western—meaning European and North American—health care; however, in other parts of the world, these alternative medicines are actually standard treatments. Some are complete systems of treatment that include different ideas about how the body works, herbal medicine, and the connection between the mind and the body.

Homeopathy was developed in Germany in the early 1800s. It's based on the idea that "like is cured by like." This means that if a large dose of a substance would create symptoms of an illness in a healthy person, a very small dose of it will cure a sick person of that illness. The concept behind vaccines is similar—when a person receives a very small or mild dose of a disease, the body can become **immune** to it.

Modern chiropractic medicine was first practiced in 1895, although there are records of the ancient Chinese performing spinal manipulations as long ago as 2700 B.C. Chiropractic medicine is based on the idea that illness can be the result of the spine being out of alignment, especially if it presses on nerve endings. To treat this, a doctor will perform adjustments, or quick thrusts that move the spine back into alignment.

Acupuncture is a form of traditional Chinese medicine that is thousands of years old. It's based on the theory that energy moves through invisible channels in the body. Very thin needles are inserted into the skin for 5 to 20 minutes to free blocked energy. Chinese herbal medicine is often used as a part of this treatment.

Western doctors have been hesitant to trust alternative medicines, partly because they have completely different **philosophies** about health and how the body works. In addition, alternative medicine can be hard to test scientifically. For example, acupuncture has been reported to be very effective in relieving pain, but this is difficult to prove because some people can tolerate more pain, and pain is hard to measure.

More and more people in the Western world are trying alternative healing, often for long-term diseases that don't respond to traditional medicine. Herbal medicine can be very powerful—about 25% of Western prescription medicines come from plants. Some Western doctors now practice **complementary medicine**, which is Western medicine used along with some alternative healing.

Write **true** or **false** next to each statement below.

1. _____ Herbal supplements are subject to the same tests and regulations that prescription medications are.

2. _____ Yoga is an ancient philosophy of health that involves stretching, breathing, and meditation.

3. _____ Acupuncture is a recently invented medical therapy.

4. _____ The types of medical treatments that Americans refer to as "alternative" may be traditional treatments in other parts of the world.

5. _____ Alternative forms of medicine and medical treatment are never effective.

6. _____ Anything labeled as being natural is guaranteed to be healthful.

7. _____ The use of herbs is often a part of acupuncture treatment.

Write your answers on the lines below.

8. What does the phrase *like is cured by like* mean? How does this concept apply to medicine?

   _____

   _____

9. Why do you think more people are willing to try alternative forms of medicine and treatment? Give at least one reason not mentioned in the selection.

   _____

   _____

10. What is the basis of chiropractic medicine?

   _____

11. What is complementary medicine? Do you believe that it's a good choice for treatment? Explain.

   _____

   _____

food-borne illnesses: any sicknesses or infections caused by eating foods that contain bacteria, viruses, or toxins

At temperatures above 40°F, some types of bacteria can double in number every 20 minutes.

More than 75 million people experience **food-borne illnesses** every year, and as many as 5,000 die as a result. Salmonella is a common food-borne illness caused by bacteria in eggs and poultry. Symptoms can include nausea, diarrhea, and vomiting.

It's a good idea to keep a small fire extinguisher within reach of the stove. In case of a kitchen fire, immediately call an adult for help. If the fire is in the oven, close the door and turn off the heat. An adult can use baking soda to extinguish grease and electrical fires. If possible, he or she can also cover the fire to cut off the supply of oxygen.

What safety and health risks are hiding in your kitchen?

The kitchen can be the source of household injuries and even illness. Here are some tips to help you stay safe in the kitchen.

General Safety

- Always wash your hands before you begin preparing any food. If you touch raw meat or eggs, wash your hands again thoroughly for at least 20 seconds, using soap, warm water, and a brisk rubbing motion.

- Don't eat unbaked cookie dough. It contains raw eggs, which can be a source of salmonella bacteria.

- Leftovers should not remain unrefrigerated for more than two hours.

- All fruits and vegetables should be washed. They can be dirty, contain bacteria, and have residues of pesticides on them. For thicker-skinned produce, like potatoes, use a stiff brush to remove the dirt.

- Foods should always be thawed in the refrigerator and never left on the counter. If left out, the outside of the food may thaw (which allows bacteria to grow) while the inside is still frozen. To speed up thawing, place the food in a plastic bag and immerse it in a bowl of cold water. Change the water every half-hour until the food is thawed. Do not re-freeze unless the food has been thoroughly cooked first.

- Color isn't always a reliable indicator, so the best way to determine if meat is fully cooked is by using a meat thermometer. Ground poultry should reach a temperature of 165°F, while other ground meats should reach 160°F. Temperatures vary for other cuts of meat but can be found in cookbooks and at the USDA food safety Web site.

Microwave Safety

- Microwave foods only in microwave-safe glass and plastic containers. Plastics that aren't intended to be used in the microwave can leach chemicals into your food or even melt.

- Be careful when removing food from the microwave. Use a potholder, and watch out for steam when you uncover the food.

- Make sure that microwaved foods are heated evenly by rotating them. If you don't, certain portions of the food might not get completely cooked and any bacteria may not be killed.

Read each item below. On the line that follows, explain why it describes an unsafe situation.

1. Alexander cut up some raw chicken and placed it in a frying pan. Then, he used the same cutting board to cut up some tomatoes for his salad.

   _____

2. Ebony took a handful of strawberries out of the carton and began eating them.

   _____

3. Gabrielle had some friends over for a party at 7:00. When they left at 10:00, she put the cheeses and deli meats that had been on the table in bags and put them back in the fridge.

   _____

4. Basir forgot that his mom asked him to defrost some salmon for dinner. An hour before dinner, he placed the salmon in a bowl on the counter to defrost.

   _____

5. Olivia and Kate made oatmeal cookies for a friend's birthday. Before they washed the bowl, they each took a spoon and scraped up a bite of dough to eat.

   _____

6. Kris wanted to heat up some leftovers from the restaurant. He wasn't sure if the container they were in was microwave safe, but it was plastic so he decided it was fine to use it.

   _____

Write your answers on the lines below.

7. What role does baking soda play in kitchen safety?

   _____

8. Why does perishable food need to be kept at temperatures of 40°F or cooler?

   _____

9. What's the best way to determine if meat is fully cooked?

   _____

Learning to Coexist

incidence: rate at which something occurs

encroaching: trespassing or advancing beyond the limits of an area

fragment: to break into parts

Wild animal attacks are uncommon, but they are possible. Mountain lions have killed joggers and hikers in California, and there have been several attacks on children by coyotes. People are advised by wildlife experts not to leave trash, food, or pet food out because it encourages unwelcome visits. In areas where sightings are common, residents are also told not to leave cats, small dogs, and young children outside unsupervised, especially at twilight.

If an animal is spotted, trying to run away isn't a good idea. This can engage the animal's predatory instincts and make it believe the human being is its prey. Making a lot of noise and trying to appear large is a better way to frighten it off.

Why are human beings having more and more encounters with wild animals?

What would you do if you saw a moose strolling up your street or an alligator taking a dip in your pool? What about a bear rummaging through your trashcan or a mountain lion climbing a tree in your neighborhood? In recent years, encounters with wild animals have been on the rise around the country. Some people are excited by the chance to get an up-close look at creatures they don't usually see, while others are concerned about the safety of their children, pets, and property.

Several factors contribute to the **incidence** of wild animal sightings in urban and suburban areas. As the human population increases, so does development. This means that human beings are **encroaching** on the land and habitat of animals. Without a buffer zone between the suburbs and wild regions, animals wander into populated areas. If they find a source of food, they will return—particularly if they're having difficulty meeting their needs in the wild because of drought or overcompetition for food.

In addition, efforts at protecting wildlife and their environments appear to be working and are increasing the numbers of many species of wild animals. In some areas of the country, changes in the land are supporting large populations of wildlife. Land that was farmland a century ago has reverted, or gone back to, its natural, forested state. All of these factors combine to make run-ins between human beings and wild animals like more likely.

One result of large populations of animals living in and near cities is that more and more of them attempt to cross roads—something that is dangerous for drivers and often fatal for the animals. Part of the problem is that roads can **fragment** a habitat or ecosystem, making it necessary for animals to cross roads and highways for access to food, water, other members of their species, and enough space to roam.

Many European countries have addressed this problem by building tunnels and overpasses to reconnect fragmented habitats. Some even contain ponds and shrubbery to create a natural environment. In the Netherlands, more than 600 tunnels have been installed in an effort to protect the European badger—an endangered animal. Currently, studies are being done in Europe that examine fragmented areas and determine where more overpasses and tunnels are needed. It's the perfect example of one way in which human beings and animals are learning to share the land and coexist.

Write your answers on the lines below.

1. Why can it be dangerous for a human being to try to run from a predatory animal?

   _____

2. What precautions can people take if they live in areas where wild animals are frequently spotted?

   _____

   _____

3. What does it mean for animal habitats to become fragmented? What role does the spread of human development play in this?

   _____

   _____

4. Explain what some countries are doing to solve the problem of fragmented habitats.

   _____

   _____

5. Give two examples of natural events that might cause wild animals to venture into populated areas.

   _____

6. Do you believe that wild animals have a right to live in areas that are populated by human beings, or should more be done to keep them at a distance? Explain your answer.

   _____

   _____

What's Next?

In the wild, peregrine falcons nest on cliffs and rocky ledges. It isn't unusual for this once-endangered species to nest in large cities these days, using the ledges of urban apartment buildings, churches, and bridges as their homes. Sixteen falcon couples currently make their homes in New York City. Do some research about these birds that mate for life and the New Yorkers who look out for them.

arson: the intentional burning of a property or an area

humidity: the amount of moisture or wetness in the atmosphere

evacuated: temporarily removed from a dangerous area

Green fuel, or living plant material, doesn't usually burn well because of the moisture it contains. However, during an extremely intense fire, the flames and high heat can dry out leaves and branches enough for them to ignite.

Fires can actually benefit the local animal population. They may have to temporarily find new places to live, but when they return, there is often fresh growth of grasses and tender shrubs to feed on. There may be less cover under which small animals, like mice, can hide, but this benefits birds of prey who can more easily spot their next meal.

How do wildfires affect nearby human and animal populations?

Wildfires can be both spectacular and frightening to witness. They are extremely powerful and can burn as much as 1,000 acres per hour. They can destroy the homes of both human beings and animals, but they can also clear the forest floor for new plant growth. A wildfire is a large, uncontrolled fire burning in a forest or brush area. It can be started naturally, as by a lightning strike, but **arson** or human carelessness are more common causes.

The conditions of the environment have a lot to do with whether or not a wildfire will take place and how far it will spread. During times of drought, especially during the spring and summer, forest fires are more likely. High temperatures and a lack of **humidity** in the air create fire-friendly conditions. High winds can also help a fire spread quickly out of control.

For many years, it was common practice to completely suppress wildfires because of the damage they caused. In more recent years, however, some controlled burns have been allowed to take place. Wildfires are part of the natural cycle of forests. Plants and trees can grow taller and stronger when there is less competition for resources like space, light, and water. A major problem that is the result of totally suppressing wildfires is the build up of fuel. Dead leaves and branches that are allowed to accumulate on the forest floor over a long period of time can create extremely hazardous conditions. When a wildfire does occur, it can quickly spiral out of control because large quantities of dry fuel are available.

One reason wildfires present so much of a problem to human beings is that urban areas and development keep spreading closer and closer to spaces that were once completely wild. People can be **evacuated**, but these new homes and businesses have to be protected from damages. Firefighters from all over the country might come to fight a single blaze and keep it from venturing too close to human populations.

Prevention of wildfires involves careful monitoring of conditions by experts. They can predict the risks and close off certain areas when necessary. Once a fire has begun, surveillance from aircraft and even satellites can give firefighters important information about the speed and direction in which a fire is moving. They may attempt backfires, which involve burning everything in an area slightly outside of the range of the wildfire. When the fire reaches this burned area, it has no fuel to feed it and dies out.

Underline the correct answer from the two choices you are given.

1. (Dead, Living) plant material doesn't usually ignite easily because it contains moisture.

2. (Fall, Winter) is one of the more likely times of year for wildfires to take place.

3. One of the most common causes of forest fires is (arson, lightning strikes).

4. Suppressing wildfires causes a(n) (decrease, increase) in the amount of fuel.

5. Wildfires tend to have long-term (benefits, harm) for plants and animals.

Write your answers on the lines below.

6. What are three examples of indicators that might predict a high hazard level for wildfires?

_____

7. Explain what a backfire is, what purpose it serves, and why it is effective.

_____

_____

_____

8. How can wildfires be beneficial for forests? Give at least two reasons.

_____

_____

9. What types of conditions can cause wildfires to spread rapidly?

_____

10. Do you think that people should be allowed to construct new developments near wooded areas that are prone to forest fires? Explain your answer.

_____

_____

11. What role do satellites have in combating forest fires?

_____

Living Way, Way Down Under

ozone layer: a layer in Earth's atmosphere that contains ozone, which is a molecule consisting of three oxygen atoms; the ozone layer makes life possible on Earth because it absorbs much of the sun's dangerous ultraviolet radiation

ice core: a long, cylindrical sample of ice

reverse osmosis: a process in which a solvent with a high concentration of solutes, or dissolved substances, is forced through a membrane in order to produce a solvent that is free of solutes

hydroponic: growing plants in a liquid rather than in soil

The average summer temperature near the south pole on Antarctica is only -18°F, but the lowest recorded temperature was -128°F during winter.

Some of the polar stations can pick up a few satellite television channels from New Zealand, while some other stations broadcast programs created by the residents.

The McMurdo Station has a bowling alley, a gymnasium, and a ceramics studio.

What is life like for scientists in Antarctica?

No people live permanently in Antarctica, but there are approximately two hundred research stations populated by scientists from all over the world. The Antarctic Treaty of 1961 established guidelines that make it the only land on Earth that doesn't belong to a single country. Although some stations were built by individual countries, many projects involve international cooperation, and the scientific discoveries are shared with the world.

What do scientists study on a continent covered in ice? The atmosphere over Antarctica is thinner than other places on Earth. This characteristic, along with the fact that the air is less polluted there, makes it an ideal place for studying the atmosphere. Earth's damaged **ozone layer**—a result of harmful chemicals polluting the atmosphere—was first discovered by scientists working in Antarctica. They launched large weather balloons into the atmosphere that carried scientific equipment designed to measure atmospheric conditions. These electronic devices sent data back down to computers located in the polar research stations, where it could be analyzed by the scientists.

Antarctica is also an excellent location for astronomers. There are nine months of polar darkness in which they can observe the stars and planets. Climatologists collect **ice core** samples with a special boring drill that removes a long, cylindrical piece of ice from the frozen ground. Like tree rings, the different layers in an ice core contain information scientists can use to study Earth's past. Tiny bubbles trapped inside each different layer are analyzed for their chemical compositions, and thousands of years' worth of atmospheric conditions are revealed.

The American McMurdo Station—Antarctica's largest—holds 1,200 residents during summer. It has dozens of buildings, including living quarters, a library, and a water plant. The water supply comes from seawater purified by **reverse osmosis**, a process that removes the salt. Fresh water is limited, so people shower only once every other day—for two minutes!

Most of the food eaten at the station is dried, canned, or frozen, but the scientists sometimes grow **hydroponic** plants. Like every other supply, though, the plants had to be shipped there by sea or by air. Living at a polar research station is challenging, but the scientists embrace the opportunity to live and work in one of the planet's most unique regions.

Circle the letter of the best answer to the question below.

1. What did scientists in Antarctica discover about the ozone layer?

    a. It contains molecules of oxygen.

    b. It absorbs ultraviolet radiation.

    c. It has been damaged by pollution.

    d. It contains freshwater ice.

Write your answers on the lines below.

2. Explain how scientists use ice cores.

    _____

    _____

3. Scientists working away from the station often get their water by breaking up chunks of ice. What does this tell you about the ice in Antarctica?

    _____

4. Why do you think the air is less polluted in Antarctica?

    _____

    _____

Unifying Concepts and Processes

1. What physical characteristic of Earth causes Antarctica to experience nine months of darkness?

    _____

2. A liquid that contains low concentrations of a substance will naturally flow into a liquid with higher concentrations until both liquids have equal concentrations. This process is called *osmosis*. Reverse osmosis uses force in order to create a pure liquid that contains none of the substance. Which physical law does reverse osmosis use force to overcome?

    _____

Acid in the Sky

alkaline: a bitter substance that has a pH of greater than 7; also referred to as *basic*

emissions: outputs or discharges of smoke and pollution, especially from a factory

Oil, natural gas, and coal are called *fossil fuels* because they come from ancient plant and animal remains pressed under layers of earth for millions of years. Because plants and animals are carbon-based life forms, burning them releases toxic carbon monoxide and carbon dioxide into the air.

Hydrangea, a flowering bush, can change color based on the pH level of the soil. In soil with a high pH and low aluminum levels, the flowers are pink. In soil with lower pH and higher aluminum levels, the flowers are blue.

How is acid rain sickening our environment?

Acid rain occurs when chemicals in the air mix with water vapor and fall to the earth. When it falls in the form of snow, fog, or even dust, it is known as acid precipitation. It sounds pretty destructive, and unfortunately, it is.

On the pH scale, which measures the concentration of hydrogen in a substance, acid rain has a pH below 7, which makes it acidic. Substances with a pH above 7, like soap, are **alkaline**. Pure water has a pH of 7 and is neutral. Rain is naturally slightly acidic and has a pH of 5.6, so any rain that tests lower on the scale is considered acid rain.

When fossil fuels are burned, smoke and pollution drift into the air. Fossil fuels are coal, oil, natural gas, and their products, such as gasoline. Their smoke contains toxic carbon gases, as well as other poisonous gases and fine particles. The biggest sources of acid rain are motor vehicles, including airplanes, and coal-burning industrial and power plants. Wind can carry acid rain hundreds of miles away.

Acid rain has devastating effects on the environment. It's particularly harsh on wildlife in lakes and streams because these environments are very sensitive to pH. All fish, amphibians, and insects will die at a pH below 4.5, and many kinds of water animals and plants need much higher levels. In forests, acid rain damages tree leaves and deposits toxic metals in the ground. People can also have breathing problems and long-term health issues from breathing pollution. In our cities, great monuments are being slowly eaten by acid rain. It oxidizes with calcite that is found in limestone and marble, creating holes in surfaces and breaking down the beautiful stone.

Researchers have been focusing on solutions to the problem of acid rain for the last 25 years. Because alkaline soils can neutralize acid rain, damage is not as serious in regions with these soils. Some energy plants clean **emissions** before releasing them, although there's still the problem of where to put the toxic waste that's been removed. Alternative energy sources such as solar and wind power can reduce our needs for coal-burning electric plants. Many people are also trying to drive less and conserve energy at home. The more people who make these efforts, the better the chances are that we'll be able to heal our environment.

Circle the letter of the best answer to each question below.

1. What causes acid rain?

   a. Burning fossil fuels

   b. Constantly changing levels of pH in the atmosphere

   c. Low levels of pH in the soil

   d. Scientists aren't sure

2. Vinegar has a pH of about 2.5, so it is

   a. alkaline.

   b. acidic.

   c. neutral.

   d. more alkaline than acid rain.

PLEASE DO NOT WRITE ON THE PAGES IN THIS BOOK. MAKE PHOTOCOPIES OF THE ONES YOU NEED.

Write your answers on the lines below.

3. What effect can acid rain have on monuments?

   _____

4. How can hydrangea flowers be an indication of a soil's pH level?

   _____

5. How would the increased use of alternative energy sources affect levels of acid rain?

   _____

   _____

6. How does soil type play a role in the effects of acid rain?

   _____

7. Explain the effects that acid rain can have on the environment.

   _____

   _____

8. If you were a lawmaker, what changes would you make to combat the harmful effects of acid rain?

   _____

From Zero to Six Billion in the Blink of an Eye

agriculture: the science and technology of growing crops, raising livestock, and farming

industrialized nations: countries that have a high standard of living due to an economy supported by a wide variety of businesses

Concerns about overpopulation are not a recent development. In 1798, Thomas Malthus wrote *An Essay on the Principles of Population*. Malthus studied a wide range of negative consequences resulting from overpopulation that are still influencing scientists today.

Much of the population explosion that occurred during the last 150 years was due to technologies that rely on fossil fuels. As supplies of these fuels shrink, some scientists wonder just how severely the world's ability to support six billion people will be affected.

Each year, the global population grows by 1.3 percent. That sounds like a small number, but it works out to 78 million more people a year— more than the entire population of New York, Florida, and Texas combined.

What caused the human population explosion?

Early human beings were hunter-gatherers that survived by following their supply of food wherever it took them. The human population was controlled much as it is in the rest of the natural world—during food shortages, the weaker members would die. Scientists estimate that Earth's entire human population at that time never exceeded five to ten million.

Then, about 10,000 years ago, human beings developed **agriculture**. Growing crops meant that food supplies became more consistent, and villages and towns began to form. People also raised larger families in order to supply the workers needed to tend the fields. By the year A.D. 1, the number of people in the world had reached about 250 million. Although the number kept rising, population growth was controlled by events such a disease, war, and famine.

Over several centuries, scientific discoveries—especially in the fields of medicine and health care—led to fewer fatal illnesses and extended the average human life span. By 1850, more than one billion people were living on Earth. At this same time in history, the citizens of **industrialized nations** began to move away from the traditional agricultural lifestyles found in rural areas. They headed to the cities and began having fewer children.

As the growth rate of populations in wealthier countries began to slow, the number of people in the poorer, mostly rural nations continued to rise quickly. Having large populations led to difficult living conditions, including food shortages and quickly-spreading diseases. After World War I, wealthier countries began sending supplies of vaccines, antibiotics, food, and clothing to help improve the quality of life in these places. Although the death rates have dropped, many people in impoverished nations continue having large families, so the population keeps soaring. Earth's human population is now more than seven billion people, with one out of every six human beings living in extreme poverty.

Population growth has put a great strain on Earth's environment and resources. The need for firewood, building materials, and farmland has caused deforestation. Burning fossil fuels pollutes the atmosphere and contributes to global warming. Scientists studying the human population are trying to determine just how many people the planet can realistically support. When we exceed that number, what will be the consequences?

Write your answers on the lines below.

1. Why did the invention of agriculture cause an increase in the human population? Give at least two reasons.

   _____

   _____

2. Why do you think people who moved to the cities began having fewer children than the people who still lived on farms?

   _____

   _____

3. How do you think the human population will be affected if we run out of fossil fuels?

   _____

   _____

4. In the United States, people are allowed to give birth to as many children as they want, and the government gives them tax credits for each child. In China, there are laws governing how many children people can have. Choose one of these policies, and then write a statement explaining why it's a good policy, followed by a statement explaining why it's not.

   _____

   _____

   _____

What's Next?

On a separate sheet of paper, draw a stick figure. Below it, draw three more stick figures to represent three children. Below each child, draw three more stick figures—a total of nine—representing a second generation of children. Repeat this pattern five more times, for a total of seven generations. This kind of exponential growth is one reason Earth's human population has risen from one billion to seven billion in just seven generations.

Review

NAME _____

Circle the letter of the best answer to each question below.

1. Alternative treatments and medicine are

   a. never used in the United States or Europe.

   b. sometimes used in combination with traditional Western medicine.

   c. not the standard or traditional form of medical treatment anywhere in the world.

   d. Both b and c

2. Ice core samples taken from the Arctic

   a. can be used by climatologists to study the climate during Earth's past.

   b. are used in reverse osmosis to create a water supply.

   c. contain little information about atmospheric conditions.

   d. are used to keep food frozen at polar research stations.

3. Which of the following is not an effective solution for dealing with acid rain?

   a. the use of hybrid cars, which consume less gasoline

   b. turning the thermostat down in the winter in order to use less heat

   c. using solar power as a source of energy

   d. creating cars that burn coal instead of gasoline

Underline the correct answer from the two choices you are given.

4. (Plaque, Gingivitis) is a form of gum disease.

5. Whole-grain cereal is an example of a (complex, simple) carbohydrate.

6. (Homeopathy, Acupuncture) is the use of very fine needles inserted in specific places around the body to free blocked energy.

7. Conditions that contribute to the spread of wildfires include (humidity, drought).

8. Researchers at polar stations can grow (hydroponic, purified) plants in order to get fresh produce.

9. A substance that has a pH of 7 is (acidic, neutral).

10. Earth's human population is greater than (6, 60) billion.

Write your answers on the lines below.

11. Plaque that builds up on the teeth can harden into _____.

12. Why is Vitamin D important to dental health?

_____

13. Why is it better to choose complex carbs over simple ones?

_____

14. Explain why you should try to avoid foods containing trans fatty acids.

_____

15. How should frozen foods be safely thawed? Explain why.

_____

_____

16. What are food-borne illnesses, and how can you avoid them?

_____

_____

17. What danger does a fragmented habitat pose for animals and for human beings?

_____

18. Why are wildfires important to the health of forests?

_____

_____

19. Why is the Antarctic a perfect place for studying astronomy?

_____

20. What are three harmful effects of acid rain?

_____

21. Give two reasons why the human population has grown so quickly in the last 150 years.

_____

Lesson 7.1   Full of Energy

geothermal: relating to Earth's internal heat; volcanoes, geysers, and hot springs are examples of geothermal activity

hydroelectric: producing electricity using the energy of water power

Scientists are constantly looking for new and renewable sources of energy. A team of researchers at the University of Massachusetts-Amherst have figured out how to convert garbage into something useful. They invented a battery that runs on bacteria. As the bacteria feed off a sugar solution, they produce electrons that power the battery. Someday, your laptop computer may be running on bacteria power.

Fossil fuels did not become widely used sources of energy until the Industrial Revolution when factories required large quantities of efficient fuel to produce energy.

Does the history of energy hold promise for the future?

Energy used as power comes in two forms—renewable and nonrenewable. Renewable energy is produced by water, wind, **geothermal** activity, and the sun. These resources can be replenished, or built up again. Nonrenewable energy, like fossil fuels, have a limited supply, and when they start to dwindle, new sources of energy will have to be found.

- The sun was the earliest and most obvious form of energy. It provided light and heat so people could hunt and survive. Once human beings discovered fire, they were able to stay in one location, survive harsh conditions, and cook their food. Another early form of energy came from animal power. Animals were used to transport people and goods, pump water, and even power machines that could saw wood.

- Around 5,500 years ago, the ancient Egyptians learned that the wind provided energy. Using sails and wind energy permitted people to travel to areas they couldn't access by land. About 2,000 years ago, it was discovered that windmills could harness wind power. The energy created can be used to pump water or produce electricity.

- In hydropower, energy comes from the force of falling water. The heavier the water is, the more inertia it has to produce energy. Ancient Greeks harnessed the power of water by building water wheels to grind wheat into flour. The first **hydroelectric** dam was built in Appleton, Wisconsin in 1882. Hydro plants can be built where a natural waterfall occurs, or an artificial dam can create a waterfall.

- Geothermal energy is trapped beneath Earth's surface. Scientists drill into Earth's crust, and the heat escapes as steam. The steam rotates a turbine, which makes electricity. Geothermal energy is limited to locations near the sources of heat.

- Energy also comes from burning nonrenewable resources like the fossil fuels—crude oil, natural gas, and coal. Because they formed over millions of years, fossil fuels are not easily replaceable. As early as 1100 B.C., the Chinese burned coal to heat their homes. Today, fossil fuels are burned to light and heat our homes and power our cars.

- Nuclear energy comes from the energy released when the nuclei of uranium isotopes, a nonrenewable resource, are split apart. The energy produced from nuclear fission is used to heat water and create steam to power turbines.

NAME _____

Match each form of energy to its description. Write the letter of your answer on the line.

1. _____ geothermal energy   **a.** produced when uranium nuclei are split apart

2. _____ hydropower   **b.** nonrenewable sources, like coal and crude oil

3. _____ nuclear fission   **c.** the use of Earth's internal heat

4. _____ wind energy   **d.** the force of falling water

5. _____ fossil fuels   **e.** renewable source, harnessed by sail and mills

Write your answers on the lines below.

6. How did the discovery of fire as an energy source change the way human beings lived?

   _____

   _____

7. What is the difference between renewable and nonrenewable sources of energy? Give one example of each.

   _____

   _____

8. What is "bacteria power"?

   _____

9. How did the Industrial Revolution influence the usage of fossil fuels? Why?

   _____

   _____

10. Why do you think that renewable sources of energy tend to be "cleaner" sources than fossil fuels?

   _____

What's Next?

Do some research on some sources of alternative energy. What are their strengths and drawbacks? How many of these sources are currently being used today? What will it take to make more of them available to wider populations of people?

The Ever-Expanding Universe

geocentric: relating to the idea of Earth as the center

Ptolemaic: referring to Ptolemy or his system of astronomy

concentric: circles or spheres sharing a common center

heliocentric: relating to the idea of the sun as the center

As important as Copernicus's work was, he wasn't actually the first person to promote a heliocentric universe. The earliest example appears in an ancient Indian text written 10,000 years ago by the scholar Yajnavalkya. He described Earth as one of several spheres orbiting a much larger sphere—the sun.

In ancient Greece, the philosopher Aristarchus suggested a heliocentric universe because he didn't believe something as large as the sun would be orbiting the much smaller Earth. During the Middle Ages, several of the great Islamic mathematicians made calculations showing that Earth most likely orbited the sun. Copernicus even cited some of their work as influences.

Who first realized that Earth isn't the center of the universe?

It's easy to understand how ancient people mistook Earth for the center of the universe. The sun, the stars, and the moon all slowly move through the sky, following the same paths night after night, year after year. From our view on Earth's surface, these objects appear to be circling our planet.

For centuries, ancient astronomers in Asia, Europe, Africa, and the Americas carefully observed the night skies. They could make amazingly accurate predictions about when and where celestial objects would appear, but the idea that Earth moved through space was beyond their understanding. They thought Earth stood still as the universe revolved around it.

In A.D. 150, the Roman astronomer Ptolemy published *Almagest*. In it, he explained his **geocentric** model of the universe in great detail. The **Ptolemaic** system places the stationary Earth at the center of several **concentric**, revolving spheres. The outermost sphere contains the stars, and each planet, the sun, and the moon are located on smaller spheres.

For the next 1,500 years, the Ptolemaic system was accepted as fact throughout Europe and the Middle East. In 1543, Nicolaus Copernicus published his groundbreaking work in mathematics and astronomy that theorized that Earth and the other planets had to be revolving around the sun. The idea that Earth and human beings weren't at the center of the universe was difficult for people to accept. It took another hundred years, and the invention of the telescope, for Copernicus's ideas about a **heliocentric** universe to be understood as the truth.

Today, we know that a heliocentric model of the universe isn't quite correct either. During the 18th and 19th centuries, astronomers slowly came to understand that our sun was just one star among many. Then, in the early 20th century, Edwin Hubble proved the existence of galaxies. Our sun wasn't just one star among billions, but the Milky Way galaxy itself was just one of billions of other galaxies.

Circle the letter of the best answer to the question below.

1. The first reference to a heliocentric universe appeared in writings from

    a. ancient Greece.

    b. ancient Islam.

    c. ancient India.

    d. ancient Egypt.

Write your answers on the lines below.

2. Explain the Ptolemaic model of the universe.

    _____

    _____

3. Why isn't a heliocentric model of the universe correct?

    _____

    _____

4. If life is proven to exist on another planet, do you think all human beings will immediately accept the discovery as fact? Why or why not?

    _____

    _____

Unifying Concepts and Processes

1. Which scientific skills were used to discover Earth's place in the universe? Give examples to support your answers.

    _____

    _____

2. Science is a never-ending process. Each new discovery builds on the discoveries made by scientists in the past. How is this selection's topic an example of the nature of science?

    _____

    _____

Renaissance Man

anatomy: the structure and makeup of an organism

dissect: to separate into pieces in order to examine

physiology: the biological study of the functions and activities of an organism

Da Vinci's journals held details of his inventions, discoveries, and theories, as well as many drawings. The writing appeared backwards in "mirror script" in many of the journals so that they would have to be decoded before they could be read.

People did not patent inventions during da Vinci's lifetime. For this reason, it's hard to be certain what historical inventions he should be credited for.

Da Vinci was fascinated with flight. He spent hours observing the flight of birds and bats, incorporating elements of their wing structure into his designs for flying machines.

What did artist Leonardo da Vinci contribute to the world of science?

Leonardo da Vinci may be best remembered as the artist of classic paintings such as the *Mona Lisa* and *The Last Supper*. He was much more than a gifted painter and sculptor, however. Da Vinci was one of the most innately curious and widely talented figures of history. He was a philosopher, musician, inventor, and scientist, with interests ranging from engineering and zoology to mathematics and geology.

Through his work as an artist, da Vinci had an extensive and detailed knowledge of human **anatomy**. He knew the structure of the body, including bones, muscles, and tendons. His understanding went far beyond what was typical for artists of his day or even modern times. As he became more established, he was allowed by several hospitals to **dissect** corpses to get a deeper knowledge of the body's structure and **physiology**. In his journals, he made detailed drawings of his findings, including organs such as the appendix that had never before been drawn. Based on his observations and drawings, da Vinci formed ideas about how systems in the body, such as the circulatory system, worked. In addition, he made similarly detailed drawings of animal anatomy so that he could do comparative studies with human anatomy.

Today, da Vinci is widely viewed as an inventor ahead of his time. He was born more than 500 years ago, and yet during his lifetime, he had the idea for contact lenses and harnessing solar power. He created designs for a helicopter, glider, tank, cannon, parachute, calculator, and many other machines and devices. Because he left such detailed notes and drawings of his inventions, it has been possible to build models in recent years.

Some of da Vinci's ideas were successful just the way they were designed—like the parachute and hang glider—while others, like the helicopter, would not have worked. Other designs seem to be missing a small but key element. Some people believe that this was intentional so that da Vinci's designs wouldn't work if they were stolen. Others believe that these elements were so obvious that da Vinci hadn't felt the need to include them in his drawings.

Modern da Vinci scholars have noted something interesting when making models of his designs. High-tech materials that are common today but would not have been available in da Vinci's time could actually make more of his inventions successful. Perhaps da Vinci really was ahead of his time after all!

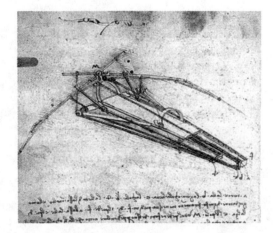

Circle the letter of the best answer to the question below.

1. What problem have people run into when creating models of da Vinci's designs?

   a. It's very difficult to read his sloppy handwriting.

   b. Some of the designs are missing a single but necessary element.

   c. None of the materials da Vinci used are still available today.

   d. None of the designs were completed.

Write your answers on the lines below.

2. How do you think da Vinci's scientific knowledge benefited him as an artist?

   _____

   _____

3. How did da Vinci record his data, scientific findings, and ideas?

   _____

4. The term *Renaissance man* is used to describe someone who has a wide variety of talents and interests. Do you think da Vinci would have been a better scientist if his interests were more narrowly focused, or does having a wide range of interests make a person a better and more well-rounded scientist? Explain.

   _____

   _____

Unifying Concepts and Processes

What was da Vinci's primary method of investigation as a scientist? Do you think it served him well, or would his time have better been spent in experimentation?

_____

_____

_____

vaccine: an injection or oral medicine that produces immunity to a disease

transfusions: transfers of blood from one person to another

Plants and herbs have been used to treat ailments throughout history. Analysis of ancient remedies (such as using honey as an antiseptic) has found that many have properties that made them effective treatments.

Major surgical advances were made in the latter half of the 20th century. The first artificial pacemaker was created in 1958, and the first heart transplant was performed in 1967.

In 1849, Elizabeth Blackwell became the first woman to earn a medical degree in the U.S. Several years later, she opened an infirmary for poor women and children. In 1868, she established a women's medical college to give other women an opportunity to study medicine and nursing.

The laser was first used in surgery in 1964. Laser surgery was a technological breakthrough because it was less invasive, which resulted in faster healing.

What have some of the most important contributions to the world of medicine been?

- Many ancient peoples believed that sickness was punishment by the gods. Hippocrates, an ancient Greek physician, helped people begin to understand that illness had natural causes.

- Avicenna, a Persian doctor, published the *Canon of Medicine* around the year 1000. It described diseases and cures and was used as a medical reference in Europe for more than 500 years.

- In 1543, Andreas Vesalius published a seven-volume book that provided the first detailed look at human anatomy. Vesalius did his research on human corpses mostly in secret. Before then, knowledge was based largely on animal anatomy.

- In 1628, Dr. William Harvey published a book proving that blood was pumped by the heart and circulated throughout the body.

- During the late 1600s, Antoni van Leeuwenhoek discovered bacteria. Most people thought it was illogical that such small organisms could cause human beings harm. Van Leeuwenhoek's work opened the door to Louis Pasteur's work on microorganisms and decay and Joseph Lister's discovery that antiseptics could increase rates of survival in surgery.

- The first successful **vaccine** was created by Edward Jenner in 1796. He found that a disease called *cowpox* could protect human beings against smallpox—a dreaded, often deadly disease.

- Before the invention of anesthesia, there was no way to block pain during surgery. Dr. Crawford Long discovered that ether gas could prevent pain. The first public demonstration of ether was by a dentist named William Morton, who is often credited with the discovery.

- Wilhelm Roentgen's experiments led to the invention of the X-ray in 1895. For the first time, the inside of the human body could be seen and diagnoses could be made without surgery.

- In 1900, Austrian doctor Karl Landsteiner realized that human beings have different blood types. This allowed **transfusions** to take place—a finding that saved many lives.

- In 1928, Alexander Fleming accidentally discovered an antibiotic called *penicillin*, which saved thousands of lives in World War II.

- The discovery of the structure of DNA—the blueprint for heredity—was a joint effort. James Watson, Francis Crick, and Maurice Wilkins were awarded the Nobel Prize for the 1953 discovery that led to an understanding of how genetic information is transmitted.

Use the words in the box to complete the sentences below.

| remedies | vaccine | transfusions | antibiotics | anesthesia |

1. _____ allowed surgeons to keep their patients from experiencing pain in surgery.

2. Many ancient _____ for sickness involved the use of plants and herbs that had special properties.

3. The discovery that human beings have different blood types allowed doctors to successfully give

    patients _____.

4. _____ were accidentally discovered by Alexander Fleming.

5. Immunity to a disease can be produced by injecting a patient with a _____.

Write your answers on the lines below.

6. What was Hippocrates's contribution to medical science?

    _____

7. How did Andreas Vesalius research human anatomy? Why was his series of books on anatomy so important?

    _____

    _____

8. What discovery did van Leeuwenhoek make? Name two other scientists whose work was based on van Leeuwenhoek's findings.

    _____

9. Why was the invention of the X-ray a significant advance in medicine?

    _____

What's Next?

What are some of the latest advances in medicine? Do some research and see what you can learn about the Human Genome Project and why scientists are trying to map the human genome. What changes could it make in the prevention and treatment of diseases?

Woman of the Trees

grassroots: a movement that begins with or utilizes common people or the people it serves

fertile: able to support plant growth

deforestation: the act of clearing forests

retain: to keep or hold in place

"The planting of trees is the planting of ideas. By starting with the simple act of planting a tree, we give hope to ourselves and to future generations."
—Wangari Maathai

Maathai is best known as an environmentalist, but she is also an activist in many other areas. She lectures about and fights for democracy, human rights, the rights of women, and world peace.

Trees combat the greenhouse effect by removing carbon from the air. They also use groundwater and release it into the atmosphere. That's why a region that is cleared of trees can become much drier.

Why is a professor helping women plant thousands of new trees across Africa?

Wangari Maathai didn't set out to change the world, the environment, or the lives of thousands of women. She has always been a high achiever, though. As the daughter of Kenyan farmers, most people probably hadn't expected Maathai's life to be very different from her parents' lives. Maathai, however, had other ideas. She earned several degrees in the sciences from American universities before returning to Africa for her Ph.D. at the University of Nairobi. She was the first woman in Eastern and Central Africa to earn such an advanced degree. After finishing her education, she became a professor of veterinary anatomy. Then, in 1977, she began the Green Belt Movement—a **grassroots** organization for which she would win the prestigious Nobel Peace Prize in 2004.

The concept of the Green Belt Movement was a simple one. Maathai wanted to help poor Kenyan women improve their circumstances in life, and she wanted to make positive changes in the environment. Maathai remembered the land of her childhood as being **fertile** and wooded. As an adult, the same land was almost desert-like. It supported fewer trees and wasn't suitable for growing food. **Deforestation** was even causing changes to local rainfall and the levels of water in the rivers. Maathai also saw the conflict that arose between people who were forced to compete for scarce resources and hoped that peace would result if competition wasn't necessary.

The logical conclusion for Maathai was to plant trees and try to restore the land to its natural state. The addition of trees would prevent soil erosion, which would also allow the ground to better **retain** water. The wood could be used in the construction of buildings and fences, as well as fuel in the form of firewood. This would mean that the women wouldn't have to walk as far to find fuel to cook their food and heat their homes. Some trees would supply fruit to supplement meals, and all the trees would provide welcome shade and green, leafy beauty.

Today, the Green Belt Movement is made up mostly of women. The organization provides African women with seedlings and instructions for growing the trees. The women are paid a small amount for each tree they plant, which also helps improve their financial situation. So far, more than 40 million trees have been added to the African landscape by the movement. Maathai is pleased with the effects, but her crusade isn't over yet—her goal is for one billion trees to be planted.

Write your answers on the lines below.

1. What problems did Maathai notice in her country? How does the Green Belt Movement address these problems?

   _____

   _____

   _____

2. What relationship does Maathai see between peace and availability of resources?

   _____

3. What are three uses that African women have for trees?

   _____

4. Why do you think it is mostly women who are a part of the Green Belt Movement?

   _____

5. In detail, explain what effect the loss of a large number of trees can have on the environment.

   _____

   _____

6. How did the Kenyan landscape change between the time Maathai was a child in the 1940s and when she began the Green Belt Movement in the late 1970s?

   _____

Unifying Concepts and Processes

Review the selection about groundwater on page 74. If groundwater is naturally part of the hydrologic cycle, why are trees a needed part of the cycle?

_____

_____

What's Next?

Do some research to learn more about Wangari Maathai and the Green Belt Movement.

Watson and Crick: Unlocking the Secrets of DNA

strand: something long and thin, like a rope or thread

zoology: the science of studying animals

hemoglobin: the protein in red blood cells that contains iron and carries oxygen

double helix: a spiral arrangement like a twisted ladder

In 1962, Watson, Crick, and Wilkins received the Nobel Prize in Medicine for this amazing discovery. Although Rosalind Franklin's work was vital to the discovery of DNA's structure, she didn't get to share in the honor of a Nobel Prize. Franklin died in 1958, and Nobel Prizes are awarded only to living people.

From 1988 to 1993, Watson was the administrator for the Human Genome Project, an attempt to identify all of the approximately 20,000–25,000 genes in human DNA.

How did competition and collaboration lead to one of the most important discoveries of the 20th century?

By the early 1950s, scientists had made several important discoveries about deoxyribonucleic acid, better known as DNA. They knew that our genes were made of DNA molecules, and that they combine to form chromosomes. The chemical components of each DNA **strand** were also known. The mystery still to be solved was DNA's structure. Top scientists in biology, chemistry, and physics raced to find the answer, but it was James Watson and Francis Crick who finally put all the pieces together.

Watson, an American, had earned two degrees in **zoology** by the time he turned 22, and was invited to join a European study of bacteria. While overseas, he met Maurice Wilkins, who was using X-rays to investigate DNA at King's College in England.

Wilkins's work convinced Watson that X-ray technology was vital to discovering DNA's structure, and he wanted to learn more about it. He transferred to the Cavendish Laboratory in England, which used X-rays to study **hemoglobin** in blood. It was there that Watson met Francis Crick. Crick, who was 12 years older, had a degree in physics, but he had also spent two years studying biology. Crick's research was driven by his desire to understand the physical and chemical processes underlying genetics.

Watson and Crick soon veered away from the hemoglobin research and teamed up to work on the puzzle of DNA structure. At the same time, Wilkins and his partner, Rosalind Franklin, continued their DNA research using X-rays. The four scientists eagerly discussed their findings, but each team was also careful not to reveal too much.

In 1953, Wilkins supplied Watson and Crick with some of Franklin's best X-rays—without her knowledge. These images were the clearest and most detailed ones yet, and they were just what Watson and Crick needed. It was obvious from the pictures that DNA's shape was a **double helix**, but exactly how the chemicals combined to create it was unknown.

Watson made cardboard models for each of the chemical components in DNA. He began playing with them, forming combinations until he saw the answer—the chemicals bonded to form each "rung" in DNA's twisted-ladder shape. After five weeks of adjusting their DNA model, Watson and Crick announced their discovery to the world in 1953.

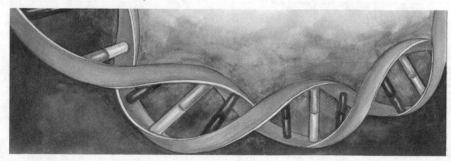

Circle the letter of the best answer to the question below.

1. Watson and Crick discovered the structure of DNA by

    a. looking through a powerful microscope.

    b. playing with cardboard models of other chemical structures.

    c. testing the iron content in hemoglobin.

    d. All of the above

Write your answers on the lines below.

2. Why was knowledge of more than one scientific discipline important in unlocking the mysteries of DNA?

    _____

    _____

3. How did Rosalind Franklin's X-rays help Watson and Crick?

    _____

4. Do you think competition among scientists helps or hurts the scientific process? Explain your answer.

    _____

    _____

    _____

What's Next?

In 1968, James Watson published the book *Double Helix*. His first-person account of discovering DNA's structure was extremely successful, but it was also controversial. Readers were shocked by Watson's aggressive and competitive personality, and the book clearly showed that scientists aren't all quiet, studious types. The book was also controversial because it barely mentioned the vital work done by Rosalind Franklin—most likely because Watson was known to be disrespectful toward the achievements of women scientists. Despite the criticism, Watson's book is considered one of the most important nonfiction books ever written. If you're interested in learning why, look for a copy at your local library.

Lighter Than Air

flammable: able to be burned

The first manned flight in a free, untethered balloon took place on November 21, 1783. Two men traveled about five and a half miles over the city of Paris. One of the passengers, Pilâtre de Rozier, was later killed in a ballooning accident while attempting to cross the English Channel.

J. A. C. Charles was the first to discover that hydrogen gas was "lighter than air" and could also cause a balloon to rise. Using gas instead of heated air to power a balloon meant that heavy fuels didn't need to be brought along. Hydrogen allowed balloons to travel farther, but it was also highly **flammable**. Eventually, helium replaced hydrogen as a less flammable choice.

Today, most hot air balloons are heated with fire produced by propane gas.

How did human beings fly more than 100 years before the Wright Brothers invented the plane?

People have always been fascinated by flight, but it wasn't until the late 1700s that human beings first figured out how to fly. It all began with a little curiosity, some observation, and a lot of experimentation on the part of two French brothers. While observing a fire one day, Joseph Montgolfier became curious about what made the sparks and smoke float upward. He began to perform some experiments to see if he could harness the power of the special floating gas that fire seemed to produce.

Joseph built a thin wooden cube and made a cover for it from some lightweight material. When he lit a fire beneath it, it rose quickly to the ceiling. Excited that his ideas seemed to be supported, Joseph and his brother Étienne began performing more experiments. They assumed that a special gas, which they dubbed *Montgolfier gas*, was causing their balloon to rise. They built larger models and finally had their first public demonstration on June 4, 1783. The balloon they made was constructed of linen lined with paper. It could hold almost 30,000 cubic feet of air and weighed approximately 500 pounds. The flight was successful and lasted about 10 minutes, covering a little more than a mile.

Spurred on by their success, the next balloon the brothers constructed, the *Aerostat Réveillon*, was even larger. While the first balloon had not held any passengers, the *Réveillon* would carry a rooster, a sheep, and a duck to test the effects of altitude on living creatures. The flight was carried out in front of the king and queen, as well as a large crowd of onlookers. The balloon reached an altitude of 1,500 feet and traveled about two miles before the animals were safely returned to the ground.

Although the flights were a success, the Montgolfier brothers hadn't actually figured out what was powering their balloons. They just knew that the balloons lifted into the air when a fire was lit. The brothers mistakenly assumed that it was the smoke that provided the lift and did their best to create dense, smoky fires using damp straw, wood, wool, and even old shoes as fuel. It wasn't discovered until 1785 that heat, not smoke, made the balloons float. By heating the air inside the envelope, it became less dense than the cooler air outside and caused the balloon to rise. The Montgolfier's "special gas" was really just hot air!

Circle the letter of the best answer to each question below.

1. Why were animals, not people, passengers in one of the first public balloon flights?

   a. No human beings had volunteered to participate.

   b. The balloon was too small to hold a person.

   c. No one was sure that living creatures could breathe at high altitudes.

   d. The Montgolfier brothers wanted to be the first passengers in a balloon.

2. Which of the following statements is not true?

   a. Hydrogen gas is highly flammable.

   b. The Montgolfier brothers were the first to use hydrogen to fuel a balloon.

   c. The first public flight of a Montgolfier balloon was a success.

   d. The most important element of "Montgolfier gas" was heat.

Write your answers on the lines below.

3. How did curiosity play a role in the Montgolfier brothers' invention of the first successful hot air balloon?

   _____

4. Explain why observation and experimentation were important to the success of the Montgolfier brothers.

   _____

   _____

5. What did the Montgolfier brothers originally think caused their balloons to float?

   _____

6. What was actually causing the balloons to float? Explain.

   _____

   _____

7. Why is propane gas a more practical method of producing heat to lift a balloon than wood fires were?

   _____

Exploring the Top of the World

What drew a high-society woman of the 1920s to the harshest climate on Earth?

When Louise Boyd was born in 1887, female scientists were rare and female explorers even more unusual. It was expected that most women would grow up to become wives or mothers, or occasionally teachers. Upon her first visit to the Arctic in 1924, however, Louise Boyd knew that such a predictable life would not be in store for her.

On a trip to the area in 1928, Boyd discovered that the explorer Roald Amundsen was missing. She led a search to find him that covered more than 10,000 miles. She was unsuccessful but was honored with an award by the Norwegian government for her efforts.

Boyd returned in 1931—this time on a scientific expedition to Greenland. She was not highly educated in the sciences but continued to gain firsthand knowledge of part of the world that was still largely uncharted territory. During her stay, she studied **fjords** and glacial formations and took photographs of local plants and animals.

Over the course of the next 11 years, Boyd led a series of these expeditions, often planning and organizing the trips and scientists herself. The American Geographical Society sponsored the last three trips, in which Boyd and her team charted the northeast coast of Greenland. During several expeditions, Boyd measured ocean depths using a sonic device. This led to her discovery of an underwater mountain ridge between two islands.

When WWII began, the U.S. government contacted Boyd as an expert on Greenland and the Arctic. She had been about to publish a book containing photographs of her expeditions, as well as data she had collected. The book could have been useful to wartime enemies, so Boyd delayed its publication and sent the material to the government. In 1941, they sponsored a trip to the region, in which Boyd studied the ways that polar magnetism affected radio communication. Transmission was not consistent in the Arctic, and it was important in a time of war that communication not break down.

At the age of 68, Boyd still wasn't finished with the Arctic. She chartered a plane and a crew and became the first woman to fly over the North Pole. The flag she carried can be seen at the Society of Women Geographers—a symbol of the woman who wasn't afraid to take risks and follow her passions in life.

Write **true** or **false** next to each statement below.

1. _____ Although Boyd did not attend college, she received many honorary degrees.

2. _____ At the age of 68, Boyd became the first person to fly over the North Pole.

3. _____ Earth's magnetic field has no effect on radio communication.

4. _____ Boyd worked only as a photographer during her time in the Arctic.

5. _____ Boyd's most valuable knowledge was gained through experience.

Write your answers on the lines below.

6. Reread the quote by Louise Boyd that appears in the sidebar. What do you think she meant?

_____

_____

7. Why didn't the government want Boyd to publish her book?

_____

8. What allowed Louise Boyd to make choices that were seen as being unusual for a woman?

_____

_____

9. How did Boyd become knowledgeable in the sciences when she didn't have a formal science education?

_____

10. What are three contributions Boyd made to the world of science?

_____

_____

11. Why was Boyd sent to study polar magnetism in the Arctic?

_____

Science's Modern Mysteries

sustain: to supply with resources that are necessary for life

efficiency: the quality of being efficient, or not wasteful

famine: a great shortage of food

essential: absolutely necessary

simultaneously: happening at the same time

Physicists have been searching for years to find one theory that combines all of the known physical laws. The Standard Model is close, showing how electromagnetic energy, quarks, and leptons work together to explain nearly every physical event occurring at the subatomic level, but gravity continues to be a problem. It's like having one tool that can measure every physical fact about an object except what color it is.

What don't we already know about science?

As you learn about science and all of the discoveries that have been made through the course of human history, it might seem as if there aren't too many mysteries left to solve. In some ways, though, the more human beings learn about how the universe works, the more mysterious it seems to get. This is partly due to the fact that the easiest questions have already been answered. But another reason is that, as the human population continues to grow, scientists are faced with new challenges due to a more crowded and complex world. Here are three examples of unanswered scientific questions. If you choose a career in biology, archaeology, ecology, or chemistry, you might help find answers for one of them.

- *What makes us human?* For many years, it was thought that the primary characteristic setting human beings apart from other animals was the use of tools. Jane Goodall's discovery that chimpanzees also use tools meant that a new definition had to be found. Today, scientists are looking closely at human DNA and comparing it to the DNA of chimps and other primates. Although we share more than 95 percent of our DNA with chimps, scientists hope to find an answer in the thousands of genes that are different.

- *How many human beings can Earth* **sustain**? By the end of this century, it's predicted that there will be 10 billion people on Earth. Advances made in food production and energy **efficiency** have allowed the human population to reach nearly six billion so far without widespread **famine**. Poverty continues to be an issue, though. There's a lot of debate among scientists as to how large the population can become before it outgrows Earth's ability to provide enough resources.

- *How did life begin on Earth?* In its earliest days, Earth was a seething stew of heat and chemicals. Somehow, these chemicals came together to form simple, single-celled organisms. These creatures eventually evolved into the complex life-forms found on our planet today. DNA and proteins are both **essential** to life, but scientists have a hard time imagining how they could have developed **simultaneously**. Experiments have shown that electricity sent through a certain mixture of gases can produce amino acids. Did lightning strike gases in Earth's atmosphere and spark the beginnings of life? Or did a meteor or comet carry microscopic organisms to Earth from another planet? There are still many different theories about how life began on Earth.

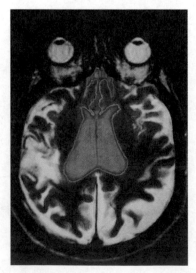

Circle the letter of the best answer to the question below.

1. Human beings share more than 95 percent of the same DNA with

   a. other mammals.

   b. chimpanzees.

   c. the first life-forms that appeared on Earth.

   d. other primates.

Write your answers on the lines below.

2. Explain how scientists created proteins in the lab, and how it helps form a theory about the origins of life on Earth.

   _____

   _____

   _____

3. What do you think will be the biggest factor in determining the maximum number of human beings that can live on Earth?

   _____

   _____

4. In the past, what did people think set human beings apart from other animals?

   _____

What's Next?

Choose one of the following questions. Then, do some research to find out what kinds of work scientists are doing on the subject and whether or not they're anywhere close to finding answers.

- When will fossil fuel supplies run out, and what alternative energy source will replace them?
- Is there a limit to how long human life spans can be extended?
- We experience life in three dimensions—four if you include time—but does the universe consist of even more dimensions that we can't sense or detect?
- Will the universe continue expanding forever, or will it stop and begin collapsing?
- Why does Earth experience ice ages?
- What is the purpose of dreaming?
- Is there an upper limit to how quickly computers can do their work?

NAME _____

Review

Circle the letter of the best answer to each question below.

1. In the 1500s, _____ published a groundbreaking work of mathematics and astronomy that theorized Earth and the other planets revolve around the sun.

   a. Aristarchus

   b. Alhazen

   c. Copernicus

   d. Galileo

2. Which of the following medical discoveries was made most recently?

   a. Human beings have several different blood types.

   b. DNA's structure is a twisting ladder shape called a double helix.

   c. Bacteria are tiny, single-celled organisms that can cause illness.

   d. Penicillin can be used as an antibiotic.

3. Which of the following statements about Louis Boyd is not true?

   a. She led a polar expedition in search of the missing explorer, Roald Amundsen.

   b. She earned her degree in geology before heading north to explore the polar regions.

   c. She charted the coast of Greenland and discovered an underwater mountain range.

   d. She was the first woman to fly over the North Pole.

Write your answers on the lines below.

4. What is hydroelectric power?

   _____

5. Is nuclear fission a renewable or nonrenewable energy source? Explain your answer.

   _____

   _____

6. Briefly describe Earth's location in the universe.

   _____

7. Name a device da Vinci imagined and sketched years before it was actually invented.

   _____

8. Choose a selection from this chapter to demonstrate how science is a collaborative effort in which each new discovery builds on previous work done by other scientists.

_____

_____

_____

9. How did Hippocrates begin to change the way people regarded illness?

_____

10. Explain why the grassroots element of Wangari Maathai's Green Belt Movement contributes to its success.

_____

11. The Montgolfier Brothers thought smoke was causing their balloon to rise. What is the real reason that hot air balloons rise?

_____

12. Name something that's still a mystery to scientists.

_____

Use the words in the box to complete the sentences below.

physiology deforestation	X-rays proteins	vaccines geothermal	fjords geocentric

13. Volcanoes, geysers, and hot springs are examples of _____ activity.

14. Ptolemy convincingly described a _____ model of the universe.

15. Da Vinci dissected human corpses to get a better understanding of _____.

16. _____ can produce immunity to certain diseases.

17. _____ can contribute to changes in climate, as well as water levels in rivers.

18. _____ taken by Rosalind Franklin revealed the shape of DNA.

19. As part of her research, Louise Boyd studied _____ and glacial formations.

20. DNA and _____ are essential for life on Earth.

Final Test

Use the words in the box to complete the sentences below.

respiration instinctual attractive	homeostasis invasive	joints magnetic	catalysts complementary	symmetrical organelles aquifers

1. A(n) _____ species is a nonnative plant or animal that causes changes to the existing populations of plants and animals in an area.

2. Proteins are long chains of amino acids that act as _____ to speed up

   _____ inside cells.

3. Gravity is a(n) _____ force that exists between any two masses.

4. Some of the cell's _____, such as the ribosomes and Golgi bodies, play a role in protein assembly and transport.

5. The human body maintains chemical and thermal equilibrium through _____.

6. _____ keep bones in alignment and allow the skeleton to move.

7. Migration is a(n) _____ journey, usually undertaken seasonally.

8. Wells tap into saturated, underground layers of rock, soil, or sand called _____.

9. Crystals are substances made up of a repeated pattern of _____ solids.

10. Fluctuations in a(n) _____ field will create an electrical current.

11. Many modern doctors practice _____ medicine, which combines alternative methods with more traditional, Western ones.

Write **true** or **false** next to each statement below.

12. _____ Scientists were surprised to discover that *Homo floresiensis*, or "the hobbit," became extinct before *Homo sapiens* appeared.

13. _____ Rates of extinction today are much higher than average historical rates.

14. _____ Parallax can be used to determine the composition of a star.

15. _____ An object that is less dense than water will displace an amount of water equal to its volume.

16. _____ Perfect vacuums are extremely rare in nature.

17. _____ A penny and bowling ball will fall at the same rate toward Earth's surface.

18. _____ Protons and neutrons are made up of even smaller particles called quarks.

19. _____ The overuse of antibiotics can lead to stronger, drug-resistant bacteria.

20. _____ Brain size is the only indicator of an animal's intelligence.

21. _____ Ice ages usually last no longer than about 50,000 years.

22. _____ Today, experts can predict exactly when and where an avalanche will occur.

23. _____ The same side of the moon always faces Earth.

24. _____ Steel is an alloy that is commonly used to build skyscrapers.

25. _____ Cell phones contain special batteries called cells.

26. _____ The sun's energy comes from nuclear fission that changes hydrogen to helium.

27. _____ Burning fossil fuels is a major cause of acid rain.

28. _____ The human population has grown at a steady rate throughout history.

Write your answers on the lines below.

29. Why are good communication skills important for scientists to have?

   _____

30. Why is it important to limit the variables in an experiment?

   _____

31. How are the ways climatologists use tree rings and ice core samples similar?

   _____

32. What is one sign that a chemical change has taken place?

   _____

33. Rust, respiration, and fire are examples of _____.

34. Name two of the three characteristics that most metals share.

   _____

Final Test

35. Explain entropy, or the second law of thermodynamics.

_____

_____

36. What is the "nature versus nurture" debate?

_____

37. Choose one form of electromagnetic energy. Describe its wavelength in comparison to another form and one way human beings use it.

_____

_____

38. Name two major threats to coniferous forests.

_____

39. How does El Niño affect the weather?

_____

40. What role does weathering play in the formation of soil?

_____

41. Explain the difference between rocks and minerals.

_____

42. Put these celestial objects in order of size: star, the moon, cluster, galaxy, Earth.

_____ _____ _____ _____ _____

43. Name two characteristics of Mars that make it highly unlikely that it can support life.

_____

44. Why is the science of cloning controversial?

_____

45. A _____ lens causes light waves to converge, and a _____ lens causes them to spread apart.

46. Choose one instrument used by meteorologists and explain how and why it works.

_____

_____

47. Name two types of foods that are good for your brain and explain why.

_____

48. Why have more wild animals been venturing into populated areas in recent years?

_____

49. If wildfires are a part of the natural cycle of forests, why do human beings fight them?

_____

50. Why was human anatomy important to Leonardo da Vinci as both an artist and a scientist?

_____

51. How does the Green Belt Movement benefit African women and the environment?

_____

Match each scientist with his or her discovery or invention. Write the letter of your choice on the line.

52. _____ Mary Leakey

53. _____ Copernicus

54. _____ Joseph Lister

55. _____ Ptolemy

56. _____ Leonardo da Vinci

57. _____ Hippocrates

58. _____ Watson, Crick,
Wilkins, & Franklin

59. _____ Elizabeth Blackwell

60. _____ Wangari Maathai

61. _____ Montgolfier brothers

a. promoted the idea that illnesses had scientific causes

b. had the first public demonstration of a hot air balloon

c. found a 1.75 million-year-old hominid skull

d. explained a geocentric model of the universe

e. discovered the structure of DNA

f. the first woman to earn a medical degree

g. discovered the usefulness of antiseptics in surgery

h. promoted a heliocentric model of the universe

i. began the Green Belt Movement in Africa

j. artist who imagined many future inventions

Page 7

1. c

2. Possible answer: You can't make a discovery if you don't see or notice it.

3. Possible answer: You should first conduct the experiment again to make sure there were no mistakes. If the results are the same, publish the results so other scientists can review them. They can design other experiments, or they might see information in the results that you missed.

4. Possible answer: A good scientist needs strong math and communication skills, as well as knowledge in his or her field of scientific study.

Page 9

1. Possible answer: It was much smaller than *Homo sapiens*, and it had a sloping forehead and thick eyebrow ridges.

2. Possible answer: They thought it would be much older. They believed that all other species of human beings had become extinct by the time *Homo sapiens* lived.

3. It was very small. The teeth were too worn for the skull to have belonged to a child.

4. Possible answer: They showed that the hobbit was intelligent and capable of problem solving.

5. Possible answer: Scientists need to be open minded in order to be able to make use of all the information available and to be able to draw conclusions. The scientists in the selection needed to revise their opinions about *Homo sapiens* being the only human species alive at a certain point in history.

6. They wanted to compare the skulls with the ancient remains to see if they matched.

7. Answers will vary.

Page 11

1. c

2. It was the first tool maker, and the name means *handy man*.

3. Possible answer: They had different strengths as scientists and as people. They complemented one another.

4. Possible answer: Having a dynamic personality helped Louis Leakey interest others in his work and get funding for it. If he had been shy, he might not have been as successful.

5. Mary's discovery of the footprints showed that *Australopithecus afarensis* could walk on two legs like modern human beings.

6. She matched them up to fossils in the area. Answers will vary.

Unifying Concepts and Processes

Possible answer: He was probably interested in the links between early human beings and primates and thought that learning more about primates could teach us about our early ancestors.

Page 13

1. false

2. true

3. false

4. true

5. When a serious search has been done over a period of time and no evidence can be found, a species is considered extinct.

6. Possible answers: ice ages, changes in sea level, changes in the salinity of oceans

7. New evidence might be found or the way it was classified might change.

8. They date and examine fossils.

9. Possible answer: An animal that eats an insect that damages a variety of plants could be beneficial.

10. Invertebrates; Possible answer: Invertebrates, like insects, may be more affected by changes in plant and animal species. Also, they are smaller and may not be as hardy as larger animals.

Page 15

1. a

2. Possible answer: The solution of alcohol and water will have the lowest freezing temperature.

3. The thermometer would read the temperature of the glass beaker, not the solution.

4. The solutions in Beakers 2 and 3 had much lower concentrations of their substances mixed in—just 6.25 percent. Beaker 4 had a much higher concentration—40 percent.

5. Possible answer: Yes. The experiment showed that equal amounts of either sugar or salt have the same effect on lowering the freezing point of water.

Page 17

1. false

2. false

3. true

4. false

5. true

6. He had surgeons wash their hands with it, cleaned surgical tools with it, and treated wounds with it after surgery.

7. He read the work of Louis Pasteur on microorganisms in living material causing decay and disease.

8. Possible answer: He believed that a very fine dust might be causing the infection. He was somewhat right, because microorganisms are similar in appearance to a very fine dust, except that they are alive.

9. The mortality rate dropped sharply after carbolic acid was introduced as an antiseptic.

Page 19

1. d

2. Possible answer: Scientists can look for patterns with other bristlecone pines to determine when each tree lived. Then, they can use the information found in the trees' rings to learn about the climate thousands of years ago.

3. He or she can learn how old the tree was, as well as learn about the temperature, weather events, and pollution during the tree's life.

4. This will allow them to gather information about the environment during the cold phase of the last ice age.

5. Possible answer: It is a state from which scientists can make something return to life after a period of time in which it was inactive and somehow preserved.

Unifying Concepts and Processes

Answers will vary.

Page 21

1. c

2. b

3. c

4. Each element emits specific colors when it's burned, so scientists know which elements a star contains by looking at the colors produced by the spectroscope.

5. Possible answer: A star that's several times more luminous than another star might be much farther away, but it would still appear brighter to us in the sky.

Page 23

1. false

2. false

3. true

4. false

5. true

6. Possible answer: It is not native to the U.S. Its introduction affected the population of blue mussels.

7. In only about 15 years, blue mussels had evolved a defense mechanism to Asian shore crabs.

8. Possible answer: Both sets of mussels were used to coexisting with green crabs. The mussels from northern Maine hadn't evolved a defense yet to the Asian shore crabs.

9. Possible answer: Because they didn't know yet that the crab was a predator, so they had no reason to thicken their shells when it was nearby

10. Possible answer: Because the mussels evolved a defense mechanism in 15 years instead of over many generations

Page 24

1. b

2. a

3. c

4. true

5. false

6. false

7. true

8. false

9. false

10. true

Page 25

11. Possible answer: Scientists need to be able to clearly communicate during scientific investigations, as well as be able to share their results with the scientific community.

12. Possible answer: A chemist would need to carefully observe the results of experiments. A zoologist studying animals in the wild would need to carefully observe their behavior.

13. Possible answer: It was very small but seemed to have a relatively high level of intelligence. No one knew that any other human species existed at the same time as *Homo sapiens*.

14. A level of intelligence and the ability to solve problems

15. Possible answer: Land is cleared for development, pollution is created, and invasive species are introduced.

16. Because there was more than one variable.

17. Yes, because it still provides information about the subject being studied.

18. Possible answer: He had surgeons wash with it, clean surgical tools with it, and treat wounds with it. He knew it was successful because mortality rates dropped.

19. He or she can learn how old the tree was, as well as learn about the temperature, weather events, and pollution during the tree's life.

20. Because the mussels evolved a defense mechanism in 15 years instead of over many generations

Page 27

1. a

2. solid, liquid, gas

3. chemical

4. chemical, because a change in color occurred

5. chemical, because an additional substance, carbon dioxide, was produced

6. physical, because the sugar changed states from solid to liquid but it remained white

7. chemical, because the sugar changed colors and emitted smoke

8. chemical, because light was produced and a change in color occurred

9. physical, because the asphalt changed from liquid to solid without any other changes

10. chemical, because an odor was produced and the substance changed colors

Page 29

1. b

2. c

3. Possible answer: No, because oxygen would not have been able to reach the copper if it was completely submerged in the vinegar.

4. Possible answer: When stainless steel oxidizes, a thin layer of chromium oxide forms on the surface. This layer prevents air or water from causing any further oxidation.

5. Possible answer: Acid speeds up the oxidation process, so monuments exposed to acid rain would rust much more quickly than they would otherwise.

Unifying Concepts and Processes

A piece of iron exposed to air and water oxidizes, meaning that iron and oxygen have a chemical reaction that forms iron oxide.

Page 31

1. a

2. c

3. They couldn't weigh the water without the beaker, but they had to subtract its weight to get the weight of the water alone.

4. 960 grams, or 0.96 kilograms

5. 1.6 kilograms per liter; The object is denser than water, so it will sink.

Answer Key

Page 33

1. c
2. b
3. Electrons move easily among the atoms of metals.
4. They are a mixture of metals or a metal and nonmetal.
5. Metal is hard and durable, and it can be easily shaped.

Page 35

1. c
2. b
3. Larger masses exert stronger gravitational forces, so gravity on Jupiter would be much stronger than on Earth.

Unifying Concepts and Processes

Earth orbits the sun, which means Earth is captured by the sun's gravitational force. Also, the sun is much larger.

Page 37

1. a
2. b
3. Possible answer: Because of the law of entropy, a vacuum is naturally filled by matter that flows from an area of higher pressure.
4. Possible answer: Water boils at a lower temperature because less energy is needed to overcome the extremely low atmospheric pressure inside a vacuum.
5. Possible answer: There are very few molecules to create friction that would affect the craft's speed.
6. Possible answer: The cork lies on the bottom because Earth's gravity would still affect it, even inside a vacuum.

Page 39

1. a
2. d
3. Possible answer: Because gravity pulled both objects to the ground at the same rate
4. Possible answer: The thrower's hand moves the ball forward. When the ball is released, inertia carries it through the air. Gravity steadily pulls the ball downward until it hits the ground. The ball keeps moving across the ground until friction slows and stops it.

Unifying Concepts and Processes

Possible answer: When a spring is compressed, it has potential energy. When a spring is released, the potential energy changes to kinetic energy as the spring returns to its original shape. Bending the pole is just like compressing a spring.

Page 41

1. b
2. a
3. c
4. Possible answer: Visible light ranges from longer red light waves to shorter violet light waves in the spectrum, so the red stop sign light waves are longer.

Unifying Concepts and Processes

Possible answer: A force is energy that can cause change. Sunlight is a form of electromagnetic radiation. It can melt ice and plays a role in photosynthesis, so it is an example of an electromagnetic force.

Page 43

1. a
2. c
3. b
4. a
5. Many particles other than protons, neutrons, and electrons had been discovered.

Page 44

1. c
2. a
3. b
4. c
5. weight; volume
6. Electrons move easily among the atoms of metals.
7. Earth's gravity pulls on all objects with the same force, regardless of size.

Page 45

8. Possible answer: Ice melting is an example of a physical change. Fire is an example of a chemical change.
9. chemical
10. The layer protects the remainder of the aluminum from oxidizing.
11. Possible answer: Inertia carries a basketball from a player's moving hands, through the air, and toward the basket. If there isn't enough inertia, gravity will pull the ball down too soon.
12. sound; radio waves; microwaves; visible light; ultraviolet light; X-rays; gamma rays
13. Gravity
14. catalyst
15. reaction
16. alloy
17. dense
18. malleable
19. gaseous
20. drag
21. electromagnetic

Page 47

1. c
2. c
3. b
4. They combine oxygen, food molecules, and enzymes to create energy.

Unifying Concepts and Processes

Possible answer: In the copper experiment, vinegar was used as a catalyst to speed up oxidation. In cells, enzymes are catalysts that speed up respiration, or oxidation inside the cell, so enzymes and vinegar play the same role.

Page 49

1. c

2. c

3. Possible answer: Bad food could poison your body, so your body's natural reaction due to homeostasis is to get the food out of your system.

4. Possible answer: No. If a cell reaches equilibrium, then no oxygen or food is going in to create energy, and no waste is going out, so the cell is no longer living.

5. Possible answer: You'd never know when your body needed to eat, drink, or sleep, so you would become unhealthy.

Unifying Concepts and Processes

Possible answer: Entropy means that two areas with different concentrations of matter will naturally mix until they are equalized, with matter always moving from higher to lower concentrations. This law is why diffusion occurs.

Page 51

1. a

2. c

3. c

4. Possible answer: The daughter inherited flexible fingers and good hearing. She used these traits for playing piano because her mother encouraged her to take lessons.

5. Identical twins share identical genes, but fraternal twins are like any other pair of siblings.

6. Possible answer: Adopted children inherit their birth parents' genes but are then raised by other people. Scientists can compare how the children are similar to or different from their birth parents and adopted parents.

Page 53

1. Fibrous

2. inflamed

3. ligaments

4. circular

5. false

6. true

7. false

8. true

9. They keep the bones in alignment and allow the skeleton to move.

10. Possible answer: A ball-and-socket joint allows circular movement and is found in the shoulder. A hinge joint allow back-and-forth movement, as in the knee.

11. Layers of cartilage allow part of the spine to bend. The lower part does not have cartilage, and the vertebrae are fused together.

12. Cartilage acts as a buffer between bones. When it wears down, bones can rub against each other, causing

inflammation and pain.

13. Possible answer: Because joints allow the body to move, and how quickly and efficiently an athlete's body moves is important

Page 55

1. false
2. true
3. true
4. false
5. Possible answer: The invention of usable, modern antibiotics depended on the contributions of at least four scientists.
6. Answers will vary.
7. Possible answer: The same concept applies to antibiotics. Overuse can lead to drug-resistant bacteria and the need for new antibiotics.
8. Possible answer: The ancient Greeks treated cuts with mold.
9. Possible answer: Many people were being wounded, and antibiotics could help cure infections.
10. Probiotics are good bacteria. They can be used for digestive health.

Page 57

1. false
2. true
3. true
4. false
5. true
6. Possible answer: Yes, because the spider doesn't have to use as much energy. It can just wait for its prey to get caught in the web.
7. Some spiders use a signal thread, which will vibrate and alert them that an insect is in the web.
8. Scientists alter their DNA so the silk gets produced in their milk.
9. Possible answer: Because spider webs are complex and very well designed

Unifying Concepts and Processes

Possible answer: Over time, spiders may have found that when they built their webs higher up, as in trees or bushes, they were able to trap flying insects.

Page 59

1. b
2. d
3. Possible answer: When one species of animal migrates, others might have to follow if they depend on that species as a source of food.
4. They can tag animals with electronic transmitters so they can track their migration.
5. Some animals have adapted to seasonal changes, and others need to move to find food or water or to escape harsh weather.
6. Possible answer: They might need to move to find a better water supply. They might be following animals that are a source of food.

Answer Key

Page 61

1. false
2. true
3. false
4. true
5. false
6. Possible answers: problem-solving abilities, use of tools, the ability to understand language and abstract concepts, a sense of self-awareness
7. Possible answer: Animals that see the mark and groom themselves know that they are seeing themselves in the mirror. They have a sense of self-awareness.
8. Possible answer: Because abstract concepts are harder to understand. They can't be learned or explained simply.
9. Possible answer: She wanted to get more fish, so she found a way to do something (hide fish to bait gulls) that would increase the number of rewards she was given.
10. They believed that only human beings used tools and made weapons.

Page 63

1. d
2. Coniferous trees have needles and cones, while deciduous trees have leaves they shed yearly and flowers instead of cones.
3. Possible answers: They have thick bark that helps them survive forest fires. They produce resin to ward off insects.
4. Clear-cutting is a logging practice in which all the trees in an area are cut down. Selective logging doesn't completely destroy animal habitat, and it doesn't wipe out whole populations of trees.
5. Possible answers: acid rain and global warming
6. Possible answer: The cones of the lodgepole pine need the heat of a forest fire to ripen the seeds and open the cones so that the seeds can be dispersed.
7. Possible answers: Use less gasoline and turn down the thermostat so that fewer fossil fuels will be burned.

Page 64

1. d
2. d
3. b
4. Most of a cell's activities are controlled by the (<u>nucleus</u>, ribosomes).
5. (Diffusion, <u>Equilibrium</u>) describes a stable, balanced system.
6. (<u>Cartilaginous</u>, Synovial) joints allow the back to bend.
7. Some people who take (probiotics, <u>antibiotics</u>) also take (<u>probiotics</u>, antibiotics) to replenish their supply of "good" bacteria.
8. Plants that have needles and cones are known as (deciduous, <u>coniferous</u>) trees.
9. Human beings have the ability to understand (<u>abstract</u>, concrete) concepts, like truth.

Page 65

10. Both use oxygen, digest food, make waste, and reproduce.

11. Plant cells need chloroplasts for photosynthesis to occur, and animals do not perform photosynthesis.

12. Possible answers: sweating when hot and shivering when cold

13. It is the question of whether heredity or environment is more important in determining who a person is.

14. A ball-and-socket joint allows circular movement, while a hinge joint allows only back-and-forth movement.

15. Possible answer: It causes pain and inflammation in the joints and can make movement difficult.

16. Possible answer: Fleming had to be observant to see what was going on in his petri dishes. He hadn't planned the experiment, and it would have been easy for him not to notice what was taking place.

17. Possible answers: They use the silk for protecting eggs and as a signal thread when an insect is in the web.

18. Possible answers: searching for food, giving birth, escaping harsh weather

19. Possible answer: Instinctual behavior is something that animals are born knowing.

20. Possible answers: the ability to make tools and weapons

Page 66

1. (Parallax, Spectroscopy) is used to determine how far away stars are.

2. Enzymes are (catalysts, organelles) that help cells make energy.

3. Most metals oxidize easily because they are (malleable, reactive).

4. Copper exposed to air will turn green because of (oxidation, conductivity).

5. The law of (inertia, entropy) states that matter always moves toward a state of balance.

6. Mitochondria, lysosomes, and vacuoles are (organelles, proteins) inside cells.

7. (Ethologists, Anthropologists) are scientists who study animal behavior.

8. false

9. true

10. true

11. true

12. true

13. false

14. true

15. true

16. false

17. true

18. true

19. true

Page 67

20. Possible answer: Some scientists believed that the hobbit was really just a *Homo sapiens* that had a condition called *microcephaly*, which made its head and body small.

21. Possible answers: in order to publish their results online and to use programs that help their research

22. They found a hominid skull in Africa that was millions of years old.

23. He had the doctors and nurses wash their hands in antiseptic solutions, and he also used antiseptics on the surgical instruments and wounds.

24. Bacteria; trees

25. odor; color change; light

26. Possible answer: A ship is shaped so that it contains a large volume of air. Air has little mass, so the ship's total density is lower than water's density. A solid chunk of iron, though, is much denser than water.

27. Possible answer: Object A has more mass because it is denser, so it will also have more force because force is mass times acceleration.

28. homeostasis

29. nature; nurture

30. Possible answers: changes in climate, finding new food sources, in order to give birth or lay eggs

Page 69

1. a

2. c

3. d

4. Possible answer: Earth is in the warmer phase of an ice age. Global warming is caused by human activity and may actually be having an effect on the natural cycles of the planet.

5. Possible answer: He found signs of glaciers in places where there were no glaciers, and this made him investigate further.

Page 71

1. b

2. c

3. b

4. Possible answer: Both are weather conditions related to air pressure and ocean temperatures. In places where El Niño causes flooding, La Niña causes drought, and vice versa.

5. Possible answer: They have close contact with the land or the ocean, and they may notice changes that scientists aren't aware of.

6. Satellite images can help scientists create maps that allow them to chart the movement of El Niños and learn more about them.

Page 73

1. d

2. a

3. Possible answer: A sluff avalanche does not contain a large amount of snow, whereas a slab avalanche can contain many layers of compressed snow.

4. Because snow doesn't build up as deeply on very steep inclines.

5. Possible answer: Because it's hard to tell if and when something might trigger an avalanche.

6. They take snowpack, temperature, and wind conditions into account.

7. Small, controlled avalanches can prevent larger, more destructive avalanches from taking place.

Page 75

1. A well taps groundwater in an (aquiclude, aquifer).

2. Water cannot pass through (an impermeable, a permeable) layer of material.

3. Human beings can access groundwater by using (<u>wells</u>, landfills) to pump the water to the surface.

4. The material in an aquifer is (irrigated, <u>saturated</u>) with water.

5. Eventually, the groundwater makes its way back up to the surface in springs, rivers, and oceans. There, it evaporates and becomes a part of the water cycle.

6. Possible answers: for household uses, in industry, in agriculture

7. The rock is too compressed and becomes impermeable deep below Earth's surface.

8. a drought or overuse of water by human beings

9. Possible answer: There may be less groundwater in Arizona, and it is probably located deeper underground. The water table is probably lower in Arizona.

Page 77

1. a

2. d

3. Possible answer: The cliff along the seashore would experience more weathering because of the additional presence of moisture and salt in the air.

4. Weathering is the physical and chemical breakdown of the matter that makes up a rock. Erosion is the movement of this matter by wind or water.

5. Possible answer: The exposed bedrock allows geologists to see layers of Earth's structure that haven't changed much due to weathering.

Unifying Concepts and Processes

Possible answer: An increase in heat will cause the rock to expand because its molecules have more energy, and therefore need more room to move around.

Page 79

1. d

2. b

3. a

4. A diamond is a mineral because it is a solid that contains one substance—carbon—and it has a crystalline structure.

5. Minerals are crystals formed out of a single element or compound. Rocks are aggregates, or combinations, of two or more minerals, and might include organic material.

Page 81

1. c

2. d

3. Possible answer: No, because gravity is the force that drew the particles together to form increasingly larger pieces of matter.

4. Quarks had to come into existence first, because atoms are made of quarks.

5. Possible answer: All matter in the universe was condensed into one point. This point exploded with incredible force and heat, sending particles spreading outward. As the matter cooled, the particles came together to form the objects in the universe.

6. Possible answer: Moons probably form in a similar way. Debris that didn't become part of a planet is captured by the planet's gravity. As this debris orbits the planet, it slowly combines to form a moon.

Page 83

1. b
2. d
3. Possible answer: Earth and its moon are made up of the same elements. Both Earth and the moon rotate on their axes.
4. Possible answers: Earth contains liquid water and an atmosphere. The moon has neither.
5. A Mars-sized object crashed into Earth several billion years ago and tore away a piece of Earth's structure. The debris was launched into orbit, and it eventually formed the moon.

Unifying Concepts and Processes

Possible answer: The moon has much less gravity and no atmosphere, so it would take much less energy to launch a spacecraft from it.

Page 85

1. d
2. b
3. c
4. Possible answer: If bacteria can travel through space on a meteorite, then it's possible that bacteria landed here on Earth and became the first life-forms on our planet.
5. They show scientists how life can survive in extreme environments like those that might be found on another planet.

Page 86

1. a
2. d
3. a
4. plate tectonics
5. Topographical
6. saturated
7. Biological
8. symmetrical
9. celestial

Page 87

10. Possible answer: An ice age is a time when there is a long-term drop in temperature and large parts of Earth's surface are covered by glaciers. They last millions of years and go through warmer and cooler phases.
11. Possible answer: They are more likely to occur on gentle or gradual slopes because that's where the deep snow accumulates.
12. Possible answers: loud noises and changes in temperature
13. Possible answer: Water falls in the form of rain or snow and seeps into the ground. Eventually, it is discharged into bodies of water, where it evaporates, condenses, and falls again as precipitation.
14. Possible answer: Underground tanks can leak, and runoff from fertilizers can soak into the ground, polluting the water in an aquifer.

15. Mechanical weathering causes rocks to break apart physically. Chemical weathering occurs when chemicals in the surrounding atmosphere react with chemicals in a rock.

16. gravity

17. It formed from pieces of Earth that were broken off during a collision with another planet-sized object.

18. All known life-forms need liquid water to survive.

Page 89

1. DNA

2. Genetic diversity

3. controversial

4. characteristics

5. Identical twins share the same set of DNA, as does a clone and its parent. A clone is created from a parent, but one twin isn't created from the other.

6. An undamaged sample of its DNA and a foster parent of a similar species need to be available.

7. A prehistoric relative of the tiger; A modern tiger could serve as the foster parent, while there are no living animals similar to a brontosaurus.

8. Possible answer: It keeps the population strong because the members have different strengths and aren't likely to be wiped out by a single disease or environmental change.

9. Possible answer: It is the changing of a plant or animal to give it new characteristics. Cloning can allow scientists to reproduce the organism in large quantities because its characteristics are desirable.

Unifying Concepts and Processes

Possible answer: No two animals or people would be exactly alike because their environments and experiences could never be quite the same. They are shaped by both their genes and environments, which would naturally produce some differences.

Page 91

1. b

2. c

3. Possible answer: If the acid didn't have enough time to corrode the copper, the lines wouldn't be very deep and they wouldn't hold ink.

4. Possible answer: Many statues are made of bronze, which is an alloy. Human beings had to discover how to make this alloy before it could be used for sculptures.

5. Possible answer: Yes. Both art and science involve problem solving, and creative thinking leads to inventive and undiscovered solutions in both fields.

Page 93

1. d

2. Possible answers: Elevators were invented, and railroads made steel and iron more widely available.

3. In a skyscraper like the John Hancock building, the outside walls help support the building and connect to the core and each other.

4. Steel or reinforced concrete poles are anchored in bedrock.

5. Wind; They build models that they can test in wind tunnels.

6. Possible answer: Stone was available. It was very strong and could withstand great pressure and weight.

Answer Key

1. c
2. b
3. c
4. A person with myopia has a lens that causes the focal point to land in front of the retina. Concave lenses in eyeglasses cause light waves to converge further back, and the focal point lands on the retina.
5. A prism bends each wavelength of color a different amount, so that white light is split up into the colors of the spectrum. A lens bends all the wavelengths of white light the same amount.

Unifying Concepts and Properties

Possible answer: Yes. We see an image in a mirror because the light waves are bent enough to send them back away from the mirror.

Page 97

1. a
2. a
3. Climatology and meteorology are both concerned with atmospheric conditions, but meteorology studies these changes in the short term and climatology in the long term.
4. As moisture evaporates from a wet thermometer, its temperature drops. Humidity is determined by comparing the temperature reading of the wet thermometer with a dry one.
5. Possible answer: The pressure is higher at sea level because there is more atmospheric weight there than up at the top of a mountain, where the atmosphere is thinner.

Unifying Concepts and Processes

Possible answer: Mercury is much denser—and thus heavier—than water, so gaseous pressure must drop significantly lower to change it from a liquid to gas.

Page 99

1. a
2. c
3. d
4. b
5. Possible answer: No. The guitar makes its own electrical currents through the fluctuations of magnetic fields created by the strings and the pickups.
6. Possible answer: An electrical current causes a magnet attached to a paper cone to vibrate. The cone vibrates as well and sends sound waves into the air.

Page 101

1. c
2. Possible answer: Because of the limited space allowed for phone calls in the spectrum, one huge tower would still be able to handle only a few calls at a time. Lots of smaller towers allow many more calls to be made.
3. Possible answer: Landline phone systems require wires to be run from every single phone in the system. Cell phone systems don't have the expense of all those wires.

Unifying Concepts and Processes

Possible answer: Smaller hardware has meant that cell phones can now contain games, music, and cameras, as well as have access to the Internet.

Page 103

1. b

2. a

3. It was developed so that researchers could share information and so that the military could have backup communication in case phone lines were down during an attack.

4. The earlier computers needed to be physically connected.

5. Possible answer: As computers became more affordable, more people bought them. Since more people owned computers, it made sense for companies to begin investing in developing the Internet.

6. By hacking into a user's e-mail address book and sending itself out to everyone listed

7. via telephone, fiber optics, satellites, and cable

8. hyperlink

Page 105

1. c

2. a

3. d

4. It's difficult to create enough energy to fuse two nuclei together and get the fusion chain reaction started.

5. Both types of reactors use heat to create steam that turns an electrical generator.

6. Possible answer: Fusion creates less dangerous radioactive waste, and the reactor doesn't need to contain as much fuel.

Page 106

1. d

2. b

3. d

4. c

5. false

6. true

7. false

8. false

9. false

10. true

Page 107

11. Possible answer: Some people think it's morally wrong to try to duplicate a living creature. They are also worried about what might happen if human beings are cloned one day.

12. Possible answer: Endangered animals could be cloned to increase their populations.

13. Possible answer: Acid reacts with copper molecules, causing the surface of the plate to become corroded. This corrosion creates pits and grooves in the surface that can hold ink.

14. It made steel and iron more available for use in construction.

15. Models of skyscrapers are built that can be tested in the tunnels to see if they can stand up to strong winds.

16. A concave lens curves inward and spreads light waves that pass through it. A convex lens is curved outward and causes light waves that pass through it to converge.

17. infrared light waves

18. Possible answer: The Internet as we know it today wasn't invented by a single person. It came about in stages, with people working together and contributing different elements to it.

19. a cell phone tower

20. Fission is the splitting of the nucleus of an unstable isotope. Fusion combines the nuclei of two atoms into a heavier nucleus.

Page 109

1. true

2. false

3. false

4. true

5. false

6. false

7. true

8. false

9. Use a straw and brush afterward or rinse with water.

10. Your body needs Vitamin D in order to absorb and use the calcium in foods.

11. fortified milk and sunlight

12. Possible answer: Bacteria react to the plaque on your teeth and form an acid that eats away at the enamel. If there is a hole in the enamel, bacteria can cause the tooth to decay.

13. People who have poor dental health have a higher risk of heart disease.

Page 111

1. c

2. d

3. Possible answer: Meal B provides berries (a source of antioxidants), fish (a source of omega-3s), and whole grains (a source of complex carbs).

4. Possible answers: fish, nuts, legumes

5. Possible answers: Complex carbs, like whole-grain cereal, are digested more slowly, so they provide the body with a steady amount of glucose over a longer period. Chocolate-chip cookies have simple carbs.

Page 113

1. false

2. true

3. false

4. true

5. false

6. false

7. true

8. Possible answer: It means that a very small dose of something that produces an illness can cure a person of the same illness. This concept is used in homeopathy and with vaccines.

9. Possible answer: The traditional treatment might not work, or they may want to try something more natural.

10. that illness can result when the spine is out of alignment

11. Complementary medicine is the combination of Western and alternative medical treatments. Answers will vary.

Page 115

Possible answers:

1. He could contaminate the tomatoes with the juices from the raw chicken.

2. The strawberries could be dirty or have pesticide residue on them and should be washed.

3. The foods shouldn't have been left unrefrigerated for more than two hours.

4. Bacteria could grow in fish defrosted at room temperature.

5. The cookie dough contains raw eggs and could cause the girls to become sick.

6. Not all plastic is microwave safe. You should never assume it is if you're not sure.

7. It can be used by an adult to put out a fire.

8. so that harmful bacteria don't grow on it

9. by measuring its internal temperature with a thermometer

Page 117

1. Because this can make the animal think that the person is its prey.

2. They shouldn't leave food or trash out, and they shouldn't let small pets or children be outside alone.

3. Possible answer: As development spreads, more roads are built, which fragments, or divides, animal habitats.

4. They are building tunnels and overpasses so that animals won't have to cross busy roads.

5. Possible answers: drought or a wildfire

6. Answers will vary.

Page 119

1. (Dead, Living) plant material doesn't usually ignite easily because it contains moisture.

2. (Fall, Winter) is one of the more likely times of year for wildfires to take place.

3. One of the most common causes of forest fires is (arson, lightning strikes).

4. Suppressing wildfires causes a(n) (decrease, increase) in the amount of fuel.

5. Wildfires tend to have long-term (benefits, harm) for plants and animals.

6. drought, high winds, lack of humidity

7. Possible answer: A backfire burns the area outside of a wildfire so that the fire can't spread. It is effective because the wildfire will not have fuel if an area has already been burned.

8. Possible answer: They clear the forest floor for new growth and keep there from being too much competition among trees for resources.

9. high winds and a lot of dry, dead wood on the forest floor

10. Answers will vary.

11. They can give firefighters information about the speed and direction a fire is moving.

Page 121

1. c
2. Possible answer: Each layer of an ice core contains air bubbles that have chemical information about a time in Earth's climate. These layers reveal thousands of years' worth of information about Earth's climate.
3. Possible answer: The ice in Antarctica is frozen fresh water.
4. Possible answer: Fewer people live in Antarctica than anywhere else on Earth, which means fewer fossil fuels or other polluting materials are used there.

Unifying Concepts and Processes

1. Earth tilts on its axis.
2. entropy

Page 123

1. a
2. b
3. It can damage them by eating away at their surfaces.
4. Their color (pink or blue) depends on the pH level of the soil.
5. Possible answer: It would cause the levels of acid rain to drop because fewer fossil fuels would be burned.
6. Alkaline soil can neutralize acid rain.
7. Possible answer: It can kill animals that make their homes in the water. It can damage plants and trees and cause people to have breathing problems.
8. Answers will vary.

Page 125

1. Possible answer: People began having more children so there were enough people to tend the crops, and the food supply was steadier so fewer people died of starvation.
2. Possible answer: They no longer needed to supply workers for tending crops, and the factories used machinery that got more work from fewer people.
3. Possible answer: Fossil fuels are burned to power farm machinery and to transport food around the world. Food shortages or distribution problems could arise and create famine.
4. Possible answer: The Chinese policy is a good way to control population growth so that there are enough resources for everyone. However, it doesn't seem right that people would lose the freedom to choose how large their families are.

Page 126

1. b
2. a
3. d
4. (Plaque, Gingivitis) is a form of gum disease.
5. Whole-grain cereal is an example of a (complex, simple) carbohydrate.
6. (Homeopathy, Acupuncture) is the use of very fine needles inserted in specific places around the body to free blocked energy.
7. Conditions that contribute to the spread of wildfires include (humidity, drought).
8. Researchers at polar stations can grow (hydroponic, purified) plants in order to get fresh produce.

9. A substance that has a pH of 7 is (acidic, <u>neutral</u>).

10. Earth's human population is greater than (<u>6</u>, 60) billion.

11. tartar

Page 127

12. It helps the body absorb calcium, which is needed to build strong bones and teeth.

13. They take longer to digest and don't give your body a big jolt of glucose all at once.

14. They can contribute to heart disease and stand in the way of peak brain performance.

15. They can be thawed in the refrigerator or in a bowl of cold water in the fridge. This prevents harmful bacteria from growing.

16. Possible answer: They are illnesses caused by eating foods that contain bacteria or viruses. Many can be prevented by washing your hands before you eat and after you touch raw meat and eggs.

17. Possible answer: Fragmented habitats can cause accidents for drivers and the deaths of animals crossing roads.

18. Possible answer: They allow new growth to take place, and they reduce the competition for resources in the forests.

19. Possible answer: There are nine months of polar darkness. There are no cities to produce lights or pollution.

20. Possible answer: Acid rain can kill animals and plants, and it can make human beings ill.

21. the development of agriculture and advances in medicine and health care

Page 129

1. c

2. d

3. a

4. e

5. b

6. It allowed them to stay in one place, survive harsh conditions, and cook their food.

7. Possible answer: Renewable sources, like wind, are unlimited and won't be used up. There is a limited supply of nonrenewable sources, like coal, so when they are used up, new sources will have to be found.

8. power created by bacteria that feed on a sugar solution and then produce electrons

9. It caused the use of fossil fuels to rise because the factories were large and needed sources of efficient power to function.

10. Possible answer: Wind and solar energy don't require that a fuel be burned, so they don't produce pollution.

Page 131

1. c

2. Possible answer: Earth is at the center of several concentric spheres that each contain one of the other celestial bodies, with the moon closest and the stars farthest away.

3. Possible answer: The sun is not at the center of the universe. It is the center of our solar system, but it just one of billions of stars in the Milky Way galaxy.

4. Answers will vary.

Unifying Concepts and Processes

1. Possible answer: Observation was used when early astronomers tracked the planets' and stars' movements. Copernicus used math to calculate the positions of objects in the solar system.

2. Possible answer: Copernicus used some of the calculations made by Islamic mathematicians to prove his theories. Copernicus published his results so other people could study them and learn that Earth revolves around the sun.

Page 133

1. b

2. Possible answer: His extensive knowledge of anatomy helped him paint and draw very realistic human figures.

3. He kept detailed journals with notes and drawings.

4. Answers will vary.

Unifying Concepts and Processes

Observation; Possible answer: It served him well because he was able to learn a great deal about anatomy. He also studied how birds fly, which allowed him to build his flying machines.

Page 135

1. Anesthesia

2. remedies

3. transfusions

4. Antibiotics

5. vaccine

6. He helped people begin thinking about the scientific causes of illness instead of viewing it as a punishment by the gods.

7. He dissected human bodies. His books were important because no other detailed images of human anatomy existed at that time.

8. He discovered microorganisms; Pasteur and Lister

9. It allowed the inside of the human body to be seen without surgery.

Page 137

1. Possible answers: The land was dry and there were few trees left. There was conflict between people over scarce resources. The Green Belt Movement provides women with tree seedlings to plant.

2. She believes that peace will be more likely when people don't have to compete to fulfill their basic needs.

3. Possible answers: fuel, shade, building material

4. Possible answers: They run the households, so they need fuel to cook and heat their homes.

5. Possible answer: It can cause the climate to become drier and levels of water to drop in rivers and streams.

6. It went from being fertile and wooded to dry and desert-like.

Unifying Concepts and Processes

Trees use groundwater and release it back into the atmosphere so that it remains a part of the water cycle.

Page 139

1. b

2. Possible answer: DNA is a molecule that plays a role in reproduction, so a scientist needs to know about both biology and chemistry to study DNA.

3. They showed the men that DNA has a double-helix shape.

4. Possible answer: It can do both. Competition might motivate scientists to work harder in order to be the first discoverer or inventor of something. But competition might also cause a scientist to withhold research, and sharing research is a vital part of scientific progress.

Page 141

1. c

2. b

3. Possible answer: Joseph was curious about what made sparks and smoke rise.

4. Possible answer: They had to perform experiments to see what conditions they needed for a balloon to float. They had to carefully observe the results so that they knew what they were doing right and what changes needed to be made.

5. smoke/Montgolfier gas

6. Hot air was causing the balloons to float because it is less dense than the cooler air outside the balloons.

7. It is easier to carry a propane tank in a balloon than it is to carry heavy or bulky fuel, like straw and wood.

Page 143

1. true

2. false

3. false

4. false

5. true

6. Possible answer: Once a scientist returns from an expedition, he or she has to organize and analyze the data that was collected.

7. The information in it could potentially be useful to wartime enemies.

8. Possible answer: She had an independent personality, she lived in a time when women were achieving all kinds of new freedoms, and her family's money allowed her to pursue her interests.

9. She learned from firsthand experience.

10. She discovered an underwater mountain ridge, contributed to the body of knowledge of Arctic plants and animals, and charted the coast of Greenland.

11. to see how it affected radio transmission

Page 145

1. b

2. Electricity added to the right combination of chemicals can result in the formation of proteins. If lightning struck these same chemicals in Earth's atmosphere, they might have created the first proteins that became part of the first living organisms.

3. Possible answer: finding a way to distribute food to people who can't grow it themselves

4. their use of tools

Page 146

1. c

2. b

3. b

4. energy created through the force of falling water

5. Possible answer: Nuclear fission is a nonrenewable source. Uranium-235 isotopes are used up in a reaction that forms two different isotopes of other elements.

6. Earth orbits the sun, which is a star in the Milky Way Galaxy, which is located in the Local Group of galaxies.

7. Possible answer: the helicopter

Page 147

8. Answers will vary.

9. He encouraged people to consider the idea that illness and disease have scientific causes.

10. Possible answer: The people who are most positively affected by the movement are the ones making the changes, so they have a lot of motivation.

11. Because the air inside them is less dense than the cooler air outside the balloon

12. Possible answer: the origins of life on Earth

13. geothermal

14. geocentric

15. physiology

16. Vaccines

17. Deforestation

18. X-rays

19. fjords

20. proteins

Page 148

1. invasive

2. catalysts; respiration

3. attractive

4. organelles

5. homeostasis

6. Joints

7. instinctual

8. aquifers

9. symmetrical

10. magnetic

11. complementary

12. false

13. true

14. false

15. false

16. true

Page 149

17. true

18. true

19. true

20. false

21. false

22. false

23. true

24. true

25. false

26. false

27. true

28. false

29. Possible answer: Scientists need to be able to clearly and precisely explain their ideas and discoveries.

30. Too many variables make it difficult to see why one result and not another was observed.

31. Both tree rings and ice core samples contain layers that show year-by-year climate changes spanning several decades, or even thousands of years.

32. Possible answer: An odor is produced.

33. oxidation

34. conductivity, reactivity, or malleability

Page 150

35. All things in the universe naturally move toward a state of equilibrium.

36. whether genetics or environment plays a bigger role in determining our personalities and abilities

37. Possible answer: Radio waves are longer than visible light waves. They can be used to carry signals so that information can be sent over long distances.

38. Possible answers: clear-cutting for development, acid rain

39. It causes heavy rains and flooding along the western coast of the Americas, and causes droughts in other parts of the world.

40. Mechanical weathering breaks rocks down into sand, which mixes with decomposed organic matter to form soil.

41. Minerals are crystallized forms of a single element or compound. Rocks contain two or more minerals.

42. the moon, Earth, star, galaxy, cluster

43. Possible answer: Mars has little atmospheric pressure, and it has no liquid water

44. Possible answer: Some people think it is morally or ethically wrong to duplicate a living creature.

45. convex, concave

Page 151

46. Possible answer: A thermometer contains mercury inside a thin tube. When the temperature rises, the mercury expands and moves up the tube.

47. Possible answer: salmon because it contains omega-3s and dairy products because they contain amino acids

48. Possible answer: Because there is no longer a buffer zone between wild areas and developed areas and because the animals may be looking for food

49. Wildfires can damage property or threaten the lives of people living in developments that are built in or near woodlands.

50. Possible answer: Understanding anatomy helped him paint realistic figures. As a scientist, learning about the structure of the body helped him understand how it functions.

51. The trees provide fuel, building materials, and a small income for the women. The climate becomes less dry, and the trees reduce carbon in the atmosphere.

52. c

53. h

54. g

55. d

56. j

57. a

58. e

59. f

60. i

61. b